The Pilgrim Pope
A Man for All People

John Paul II's Visits to the U.S.A.,
Mexico, Poland, and Ireland

Francis X. Murphy, C.SS.R.

Our Sunday Visitor, Inc.
Huntington, Indiana

ACKNOWLEDGMENTS

The preparation of this book has been a collective effort by the staff of Shepherd Press, who worked around the clock during the pope's visit to the United States. Without the guidance of Father Francis X. Murphy, who graciously contributed his experience and skills, this book would not have been possible. The writers who collaborated with Father Murphy were Michael Greene and John Vance. We also gratefully acknowledge the valuable help given by the Reverend Michael J. Roach and the Reverend Herbert Derwart.

Photos by: Jonathan Atkin, Paul Framer, John Zierten, P. A. Interpress, Religious News Service, L'Osservatore Romano, and United Press International, Inc.

ISBN 0-87973-670-4

Library of Congress Catalog Card Number 79-67391

Copublished by Our Sunday Visitor, Inc., 200 Noll Plaza, Huntington, Indiana 46750, and Shepherd Press, 30 Ruta Court, South Hackensack, New Jersey 07606

Manufactured in the United States of America

CONTENTS

Introduction

A Review

INTRODUCTION

In the course of its bimillenial history, the Catholic Church has startled the world on innumerable occasions. In scriptural terms, it is continually producing from its vast storehouse of people and experiences old things and new. During the last year, the church has produced not one but two new popes, the first of whom, an Italian from Venice, promised to write a new page of papal history. But before he could do more than set out the symbols of a new style of pontifical rule—he abolished the centuries-old coronation ceremonies, the tiara, and the throne—he was gone. John Paul I lasted but thirty-three days.

His successor, John Paul II, elected by a stunned 110 cardinals in two brief days of balloting, proved to be a new turn in papal history. After 455 years of Italian dominance in the papacy, the new Holy Father was a Pole from Krakow, and as popes go, a young man of fifty-eight, full of vigor and *joie de vivre*.

Every bit as much of a traditionalist churchman as his predecessors, the Polish pontiff immediately demonstrated an independence of activity that would mark his pontificate as a truly pastoral experience. His choice of the name John Paul II brought him the goodwill of a world that loved John XXIII, admired Paul VI, and was about to take John Paul I warmly to its heart.

Pope John Paul's genius combines a charismatic gift of youthful vigor, human warmth, a clear, logical apperception of religious and political truths, and the mind-set of a compassionate but conservatorial churchman.

In his public utterances, John Paul II has revealed a remarkable dichotomy of convictions. In the political realm, where he justifies the church's involvement on the score of its custodianship of human rights, he is definitely dedicated to the pursuit of justice and the eradication of exploitation and terrorism.

But as a custodian of the church's traditions of truth in the doctrinal and moral realm, he is an uncompromising assertor of God's revelation. He is concerned with the inviolability of man's and woman's dignity as made in God's image, and the obligation of each individual to acknowledge his or her debt to God's and the church's respect for human life in all its aspects.

Few popes in the whole course of their reigns have made an impression on the contemporary world as John Paul II has in the first year of his pontificate. "Sto lat!" May he live a hundred—or by his own request—at least ten years!

F. X. Murphy, C.SS.R.
Holy Redeemer College
Washington, D.C.

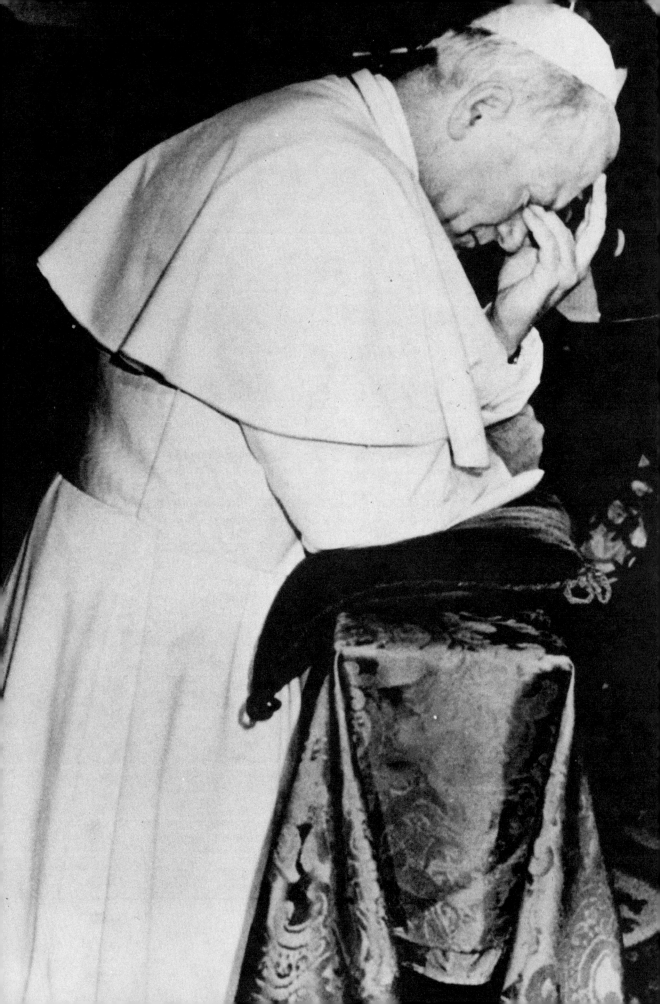

1

AFTER THE ELECTION

As a pilgrim confronting today's world, the pope from Poland, John Paul II, takes his place in a long line of traveling pontiffs beginning with Saint Peter. For the mountaineer from Krakow is not unlike the fisherman of Galilee, "a man from afar" who journeyed from Jerusalem to the Eternal City to become the first bishop of Rome.

Throughout history, popes have been on the road almost as much as they have been at home in Rome. Medieval popes traveled to northern Italy, Gaul, and Germany spreading the Word of God in a quest for peace. Only with the abolition of the Papal States in 1870 did the pontiffs voluntarily wall themselves in the Vatican as virtual prisoners. While Pope Pius XII motored down to Castel Gandolfo occasionally during the heat of summer, it was Pope John XXIII who returned to the road as a pilgrim. He visited the Byzantine monastery at Grottaferrata, nearby churches and Marian Shrines, and traveled by railroad to the "Holy House" at Loretto in northern Italy.

With Paul VI, the image of the pope as a world traveler and pilgrim came into focus. Going out among the people, his first pilgrimage was, properly, to Jerusalem and the Holy Land. He became the first pope ever to visit Latin America and the United States and to speak before the United Nations. He traveled elsewhere, too, taking pride in referring to himself as a "pilgrim pope."

When Karol Cardinal Wojtyla of Poland was raised to the papacy on October 16, 1978, he expressed his great respect for John XXIII and Paul VI, two of the most important and venerated popes of all time. Paul VI was especially close to his heart as a man, a religious thinker, and as an actively involved pontiff. He was particularly impressed by Paul VI's concept of the pope as pilgrim and quickly revealed his determination to continue in that role, carrying the mantle of the Holy See to as many people and countries as possible.

Almost immediately after taking office, John Paul II announced he was ready and willing to travel anywhere in the world. In addition to his native Poland, he mentioned wanting to visit the Soviet Union, Egypt, Lebanon, Ireland, Latin America, and the United States. In the main, these are areas of political and religious conflict: Poland, an island of continuing Catholic endeavor within a sea of atheistic authority; Mexico

A solemn time for the pontiff at La Mentorella, a tiny mountaintop church in Italy maintained by a Polish religious order.

with its anticlerical constitution and government; the war-torn countries of Ireland and Lebanon. It was clear that the pope felt it his pastoral duty to offer to these strife-ridden nations the message of peace inherent in Christianity and that he regarded the church as the embodiment of that peace and himself as its messenger.

Besides his world-pastoral mission, the new pope had to confront problems in internal church affairs. For instance, there had been a continual falling off of those interested in becoming priests. Moreover, within the ranks had developed a definite and often bitter split between liberal and conservative elements. In addition, close relationships between the Vatican and several states, notably Spain and Ireland, were no longer to be taken for granted. In short, the church needed new direction and looked to John Paul II to supply it.

A NEW ERA

The election of a Polish cardinal as pope on October 16, 1978, came as a complete surprise to the world. When TV cameramen and reporters from Poland came the following day to cover the event, journalists who had been covering the conclave joked with them for arriving so late. The excuse: "We had no idea that a Pole would make it!" Few others did, either.

Early balloting suggested that either the conservative cardinal of Genoa, Giuseppe Siri, or a former aide to Pope Paul VI, Giovanni Cardinal Benelli of Florence, would be the choice. The picture changed with subsequent voting, however, and on the eighth ballot, Karol Cardinal Wojtyla, archbishop of Krakow, emerged with over ninety votes, far more than were needed to ensure his election.

In their switch to Karol Wojtyla, the cardinals had given little thought to the political implications of choosing a pope from behind the Iron Curtain. Indeed, few of them had a specific candidate in mind when entering the conclave, and there was only a mild amount of electioneering despite all the press speculation about "politics" behind the scene.

Representatives of the news media were as surprised as everyone else by the outcome. The result: a frantic need for instant biographical information. They discovered that the new pope was known as a man of culture

John Paul assumes his duties as bishop of Rome by taking formal possession of his throne at the basilica of Saint John Lateran.

and quiet ways, a working poet as well as a philosopher. This reputation had influenced the Polish government leaders to accept him as archbishop of Krakow in 1964; they hoped he might counter the intransigence of Stefan Cardinal Wyszynski, the chief prelate of Poland. They soon found, however, that Cardinal Wojtyla could be equally difficult in dealing with the government. His mettle was demonstrated in a ten-year struggle to force the authorities to allow the construction of a church in Nowa Huta, the modern, government-planned and developed industrial city outside Krakow. A church, the government felt, had no place in an environment inspired and created by an atheistic socialist doctrine. In the end, however, Karol Wojtyla won, and the huge, futuristic edifice now adorns the city.

The press also learned that the new pope, as bishop and theologian, had been deeply involved in preparations for Vatican Council II. He had contributed significantly to the revolutionary changes that the council produced and then concentrated on adapting this teaching to the needs of today's world. His approach to problems of love, marriage, religious freedom, and culture was deeply humane and understanding, demonstrating the need to comprehend the actualities of a situation before seeking Gospel-based solutions to moral dilemmas. In the 1950s, as a young bishop, he had published a book entitled *Love and Responsibility,* which was remarkable for its up-to-date, realistic discussion of the physiological, psychological, and moral issues posed by love, sex, childbirth, and birth control. So factual was the discussion that the book may well have been responsible for the unfounded rumor

*An infant is baptized
by the Holy Father.*

that the pope had been married and widowed
before entering the priesthood.

Still, for every question that could be
answered about the new pope, there were
many others to which only his words and
deeds could supply answers. The world
waited for them. Perhaps the waiting was
most intense among the people most
intimately bound by history and geography
to the papacy, the people of Italy. What could
they expect from this man, the first non-
Italian pope in centuries? The Holy Father's
immediate, tradition-breaking assurance to
Romans and the world that he would do his
best to speak "your — no, *our*" (the slip
seemed deliberate) "language," won him
spontaneous and universal acceptance.

As bishop of Rome, Pope John Paul II
addressed himself quickly to the myriad
problems facing the Italian church. In Italy
(as elsewhere), attitudes and laws regarding
divorce, abortion, homosexuality, and
women's rights are in flux, and the pope
created controversy by reaffirming traditional
positions on these issues. Indeed, in his
first public appearances, he sounded quite
conservative as he stressed the beauty of
motherhood to 15,000 young women, advised
priests and nuns to wear clerical garb in
public, and ignored the suggestion of
the Anglican primate, Donald Coggan,
present for the pope's installation, that he
immediately declare intercommunion between
the Catholic and Anglican churches.

As might be expected, opposition leaders
in the Italian Parliament tried to label the
Holy Father's condemnation of divorce and
abortion as interference in Italian politics;
but the pope was not intimidated by that

ploy. Indeed, he knew, better than anyone,
how baseless the charge was. Shortly after
his election, John Paul II assured an audience
of ambassadors, ministers, and personal
representatives of governments accredited
to the Holy See that the church had no
desire for special treatment by states or any
intention of meddling in politics. Thus, he
did not interfere in negotiations between the
Italian government and the Vatican to
revise the Concordat reached in 1929 with
Mussolini's Fascist regime. When these
negotiations produced a document providing
for disestablishing the Catholic church in Italy,
freedom of conscience, civil marriage,
the abolition of special privileges for the
clergy, and the end of obligatory religious
instruction in schools, the pope quickly
agreed to it despite violent opposition by
some arch-conservative Catholics and
superannuated members of the papal
household, but with the blessing of the
majority of Italian bishops.

A similar situation existed in Spain,
where a new constitution was voted in during
the last month of 1978. Although it was
attacked as "agnostic" and even "atheistic" by
some, a Vatican legal expert commented that
"the Constitution contains nothing a Christian
conscience should reject." This remark
seemed inspired by the new pope's conviction
that old-style conflicts between church and
state were passé.

But this by no means implied that the
church was to be subservient to the state.
From the beginning, Pope John Paul II
demanded freedom for the church to conduct
its own affairs in its own way on its own
terms. When the pontiff's 1978 Christian
message to Krakow was senselessly mutilated
by a local censor, who removed the Holy
Father's reference to Saint Stanislaus,
Poland's patron saint, as a champion of liberty,
John Paul reacted quickly. The following
Sunday, an indignant pope blasted the Polish
regime in his midday appearance at his
window and ordered the powerful Vatican
radio to turn its attention to Poland.

Those around him had quickly
discovered that John Paul II's papacy would
be energetic. He was up by 5:00 A.M. every
day. After his morning prayers, before
breakfast, he would study a foreign language,
work at his desk, catch up on current affairs,
or prime himself for a meeting with a foreign
dignitary. After breakfasting with colleagues

(he doesn't like eating alone) and going over the day's schedule, John Paul would devote most of his time to giving audiences. He never seemed to tire of meeting people, surprising admirers who had met him previously by recalling some detail they never expected him to remember. Vatican aides and officials noticed that his audiences lasted much longer than scheduled. He constantly broke through formalities to mix informally with Vatican visitors regardless of their status. The hard work involved in greeting people, acknowledging their efforts to get close to him, replying to their good wishes in several languages, seemed to give this hearty, physically fit man strength. Only at the end of extremely taxing and demanding exertions did he show a modicum of fatigue. It quickly became apparent that the new pope's energy and endurance were phenomenal.

OCTOBER 29, 1978: AN ITALIAN PILGRIMAGE

The night of his election, the Holy Father told the Italians in his audience that he would be an Italian pope as well as a Slavic one. He assured them that by becoming pope he also became Roman. After all, as pope, he is head of a state located in Italy. Moreover, he is officially the bishop of Rome, an office whose importance he intended to stress after

Having some fun with schoolchildren, John Paul shields his ears from their deafening cheers.

years of apparent neglect in the pontiff's storehouse of titles.

As an Italian, the pope decided to start his papal pilgrimages among the Italian people. On the Sunday afternoon of October 29, 1978, he flew by helicopter from the Vatican to a small chapel atop Mount Guadagnolo, twenty miles east of Rome.

This chapel had special significance for John Paul II, for he had gone there often while on official visits from Rome in his duties as archbishop of Krakow. Not only did he enjoy communion and fellowship with the Polish monks who maintain a small church, but Mount Guadagnolo also afforded him the opportunity to keep up his mountain-climbing skills. It was there he had come to meditate a week before his election.

Along with thousands of people who had climbed up to the church with him, John Paul knelt before an antique wooden statue of the Virgin Mary, to whom the church is dedicated, and then attended a Mass celebrated by Bishop Guglielmo Giaquinta of Tivoli.

Following this visit, it was announced that John Paul would continue his Italian pilgrimage the next Sunday by visiting Assisi and the Shrine of Saint Catherine in Rome.

With outstretched hands, His Holiness blesses the people in [Sai]nt Francis Square.

The pope with one of his personal secretaries, Father John Magee, at Castel Gandolfo.

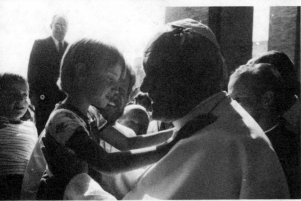

Above: John Paul holds a young boy for a moment. Right: His Holiness with Alessandro Pertini, president of Italy.

NOVEMBER 5, 1978:
ASSISI AND SAINT CATHERINE OF SIENA

Flying to Assisi by helicopter on Sunday morning, November 5, John Paul visited the birthplace of the principal saint of Italy, Saint Francis. At this world-renowned saint's crypt, the pope knelt in silence, then quietly, humbly, and sincerely prayed, "Help me, O Saint Francis of Assisi, to bring Christ closer to the church and to the world." Greeting the thousands of faithful who turned out for the occasion, he asked them to adopt in their lives the poverty and simplicity of this most lovable of saints.

That afternoon, after returning to the Vatican, he went by limousine to the Shrine of Saint Catherine of Siena, Italy's other great patron saint, located in the basilica of Saint Mary Sopra Minerva in the center of old Rome. Five thousand people were on hand as the pope entered their midst to shake hands, greet children, and enjoy general fellowship with one and all. During this pilgrimage the Roman police complained about the risks involved in the pope's mingling so close to the people. The recent epidemic of terrorism in Italy had them extremely concerned over his safety in any crowded situation. Their worry was duly appreciated by John Paul, but he politely ignored their advice, enjoying several close encounters with the crowds before returning to the solitary safety of his apartments in the Vatican.

NOVEMBER 12, 1978:
SAINT JOHN LATERAN IN ROME

The basilica of Saint John Lateran in Rome is the pope's cathedral as bishop of Rome. The church and adjacent buildings are erected on property given to the papacy by the Emperor Constantine, after his conversion in the early part of the fourth century, to be the pope's official residence. It was used as such down to modern times. Though concerned about the spiritual and civil conditions of the Eternal City, recent popes found little time to oversee its pastoral needs. John Paul decided to take a more active part in the administration of this diocese. After taking formal possession of the Lateran Basilica on November 12, 1978, in ceremonies going all the way back to early medieval times, he promised Cardinal Ugo Poletti, acting as

the pope's vicar for the Roman diocese, that he would spend some time each month in the basilica giving guidance for the rejuvenation of the church's activities among the Roman faithful. During the following weeks, John Paul returned to a practice begun by Pope John XXIII. Each Sunday he visited a different parish, either within the city or in its vast environs, slowly motoring through the neighborhood, then saying Mass and preaching to the people. He thus carried out his function as Rome's bishop, overseeing the spiritual life of his faithful.

In a historic meeting at the Capitolium, Rome's ancient City Hall, the pope met with Giulio Argan, the Communist mayor of Rome. The Polish pope, following the example of Paul VI, assured this official that the Holy Father would do everything possible to restore a spirit of Romanita — benevolent law and order — to the city, helping provide lodging for the homeless, work for the unemployed, and a sense of pride in the Eternal City as a world capital.

DECEMBER 17, 1978: MEETING THE SCHOOLCHILDREN OF ROME

On December 17, 1978, John Paul met with 50,000 Roman schoolchildren who had gathered for an audience with him beneath his apartment windows overlooking Saint Peter's Square. On this occasion, the children had come to sing him Christmas carols and to have him bless the baby Jesus dolls they were to use in the nativity scenes in their homes. The pope was enchanted by the children and joined them in singing their carols; then he sang a carol in Polish for them, teaching it to them as he went along.

Besides his regular Wednesday audiences in the new hall of audiences renamed after Paul VI, John Paul started a series of meetings with youths and teenagers each Wednesday morning in Saint Peter's. He likewise reached out to welcome other special groups on anniversaries and particular occasions.

The pope prays at the tomb of Saint Francis of Assisi.

2

THE MEXICAN CONFERENCE

After his election in late October, 1978, Pope John Paul II found his desk crowded with invitations to visit every corner of the world. Perhaps the most pressing was a request that he attend the Latin American Bishops' Conference in Puebla, Mexico.

Postponed twice by the deaths of popes Paul VI and John Paul I, the Puebla meeting was to review what had happened to the Latin American church in the ten years since the great 1968 conference at Medellin, Colombia. This meeting had produced the famous "Medellin Manifesto," which proclaimed to the world that the church of Central and South America was no longer to be identified with the rich and the powerful. Instead, bishops and priests, nuns and lay activists were to preach and teach by living close to the people, fighting the government oppression, economic injustice, and social exploitation that have reduced so many millions of Latin Americans to misery and despair.

This program, expressing what was called the "theology of liberation," was blessed by Pope Paul VI, who attended the Medellin meeting, and put into effect by the clergy and laity of the Latin American church. Yet there was opposition, largely from old-fashioned churchmen, some well-to-do lay people, and political leaders who feared large-scale social and political change. These same groups had reservations about the Puebla meeting.

As archbishop of Kraków, Karol Cardinal Wojtyla was aware of preparations for the meeting and of the controversy surrounding it. One of his first acts as pope was to authorize the Puebla conference for early 1979. It was to open on January 28 and continue through February 13.

But should His Holiness attend the conference? Some conservative churchmen opposed the trip. Others, like Archbishop Helder Camara of Recife, Brazil, urged the Holy Father to encourage Latin American Catholics with his first overseas pilgrimage. Pope John Paul II decided to go to Mexico.

On the morning of January 25, 1979, the supreme pontiff left Rome aboard an Alitalia DC-10. As he told reporters during the flight, he was following the route taken by Columbus and the early explorers in

Wearing a Mexican sombrero, Pope John Paul II makes friends with a youngster during his visit to Cuilapan, an Indian village near Oaxaca.

reaching the New World. Though safer, faster, more comfortable, and certainly more thoroughly planned than the voyages of those ancient mariners, the trip was still an adventure for this newly elected pope.

Mexico has had a long history of conflict between church and state. Catholicism was brought to Mexico by the Spanish conquistador Hernando Cortés in 1521; ever since, some Mexicans have sought to identify it with oppression. This was especially noticeable during Mexico's fight for independence in 1821, the presidency of Benito Juárez during the 1850s, the dictatorship of Porfirio Diaz and the resulting Revolution of 1910, and the persecutions and purges suffered by the church at the hands of the state during the 1920s and 1930s.

It continues today, for the Mexican Constitution, drawn up by the revolutionary regime of 1917, remains glaringly antichurch. It bars the church from participating in the educational process; it declares state ownership of all church buildings; it prohibits outsiders from becoming priests; it forbids priests and nuns to wear their habits outside the church; and it establishes penalties against church involvement in politics.

In recent years, however, this conflict has lain dormant. In 1940, the administration of President Manuel Ávila Camacho, a practicing Catholic, initiated a modus vivendi — a détente — with the church that has lasted up to the present administration of President López Portillo. During this time, various administrations, without rescinding the antichurch prohibitions set down in the Constitution, have not been strict about enforcing them or punishing violations, leaving the church relatively free to carry on its mission. Nevertheless, during the pope's visit, the government refused to recognize Vatican diplomatic credentials, thereby forcing His Holiness into the role of "distinguished visitor" without an official government invitation. The only dispensation from the antichurch laws they offered the pope was to allow him to wear his papal robes in public.

Moreover, there was concern about the pope's attending the Puebla conference because of internal church conflict over the "theology of liberation," a position set forth in the declaration of the Second Latin

An exuberant John Paul II, with arms outstretched, greets a welcoming throng of thousands as he arrives in Mexico City on January 26.

10

American Bishops' Conference, held in 1968.

In spite of these omens, Pope John Paul II enthusiastically embarked on his first overseas trip as a "pilgrim pope," referring to himself as a "traveler of peace and hope."

THE DOMINICAN REPUBLIC

The plane landed during the afternoon of January 25 in Santo Domingo, the capital of the Dominican Republic. It was a fitting preliminary to the pope's New World pilgrimage, for it was on this island that the first Catholic Mass ever celebrated in the New World was said. Here, too, stands the oldest cathedral in the Americas, Santa Maria la Menor, a limestone edifice begun in 1521, the year of the Mexican conquest, and finished in 1535. The cathedral had the added distinction of housing in its crypt what are purported to be the bones of Christopher Columbus.

After a welcome at the airport from Dominican president Antonio Guzmán, the papal party journeyed to Santo Domingo's Plaza de la Independencia, where the pope conducted a Mass before 250,000 Dominicans. He said the entire Mass in Spanish, a language he had mastered only a few weeks before in the early-morning hours preceding his busy Vatican workdays.

MEXICO CITY

Millions of Mexicans lined the fences and roads around the Mexico City International Airport as the pope's plane touched down the morning of January 26. The occasion was made even more festive by the presence of lively brass bands, guitar-strumming, malaguena-crooning troubadours, plus dozens of mariachi bands, those musical aggregations whose distinctive instrumentation and musical style is uniquely Mexican.

At the sight of the pope, the 10,000 admirers allowed inside the airport proper moved forward as if each one craved personal contact with him. One such admirer managed to place a sombrero on the pope's head, where it stayed until after he had taken his

Pope John Paul II greets bishops attending a pontifical Mass at the Palafoxana Seminary in Puebla.

John Paul II with Antonio Guzmán, president of the Dominican Republic, and his wife.

seat in the open-air bus that carried him the fifteen miles into Mexico City.

At 4:10 that morning, Mexico City had been rocked awake by an earth tremor that had registered 6.3 on the Richter scale. Smaller tremors continued throughout the day. These earthquakes are symbolic of the character of both the land and the people. Geographically, most of Mexico lies between two massive, craggy mountain ranges, the Sierra Madre Occidental on the west and the Sierra Madre Oriental on the east. These are volcanic ranges whose main peaks still fume threats at the sky and are responsible for separating and isolating so much of the country's population.

Mexico's climate and topography represent a ferocious mixture of extremes, ranging from seething tropical rain forests to barren, calcine-dry, forbidding deserts. Rainfall is cruelly inconsistent, starving the northern and central areas while drowning the tropical areas in the south. As a result, only 7 percent of the land is arable.

So dramatic a climate and environment have given birth to a people whose history and suffering are equally dramatic. Three types of people dwell in Mexico. There are

Security men help deflect a hail of falling confetti tossed to John Paul II on his way to the Third General Conference of Latin American Bishops at Puebla.

the "Spanish," that is, persons of Spanish heritage born in Mexico. They make up 10 percent of the population and reside mainly in the large urban areas as members of the middle and upper classes. Second, there are the Indians, whose heritage goes back to civilizations active before and up to the time of the conquest by the Spanish conquistadores. They constitute 30 percent of the population and generally stay, as one writer has put it, "dissolved into the landscape." The mestizos, those of mixed Spanish and Indian blood, make up 60 percent of the population and constitute the true face of Mexican humanity.

It was in the main these people, "begotten with violence and without joy," as the Mexican author Fernando Benitez describes them, whom the pope met on this pilgrimage. They have been characterized as aggressive, distrustful, aloof, and volatile but also extremely religious and devoutly Catholic. Forbearance is a trait they respect and one that all their heroes must exhibit.

The majority of mestizos are referred to as *pelados* — "the marginal, the refugee of the city, a type," according to Samuel Ramos, who has written a definitive book on the Mexican character, "economically less than a proletarian

Wearing a colorful handwoven serape, the pope receives flowers from a young ranchero.

and intellectually a primitive." The *pelados* and the Indians are the poor of Mexico, who live in utter squalor that cries out pathetically for compassion as soon as someone turns up the slabs of patriotic marble and modern concrete under which it is hidden.

It was this poverty that, in a way, became the focus of the pope's trip, especially in the aftermath of some remarks he made at the Puebla conference.

The first two days of Pope John Paul II's Mexican pilgrimage, however, were spent in the Federal District, or Mexico City. In this impressively continental city of 5 million, with its intriguing and splendid history, its wide boulevards, its blending of Spanish colonial and modern architecture into a cosmopolitan whole, the pope paraded, visited, and celebrated among the curious and festive throngs that followed him about. He met with the clergy. He visited the city's Polish colony, where he sang, danced, and ate with his traditionally costumed national relatives. He met with nuns. He smiled, he opened his arms to the people, and he was accepted reverently.

He said a Mass in the Metropolitan Cathedral, a ponderous, baroque edifice built of stone on the site of a former Aztec temple and located in the heart of the old city on one of the world's largest plazas, called the Zócalo.

After the Mass, he visited the shrine of *la Virgin Morena*, the Virgin of Guadalupe, the most sacred symbol of Mexico. In the year 1531, the story has it, the Virgin Mary appeared as a dark-skinned Indian in a vision before the Indian Juan Diego and told him she was the Holy Mother of the true God and that he was to tell the bishop of Mexico to build her a temple on that very spot. The complex of buildings erected there, including two churches, was raised to the status of a basilica by the Church in 1904.

PUEBLA

On Sunday, January 28, Pope John Paul II went by motorcade up and across the behemothlike mountain range in whose midst rise the two most famous mountains in Mexico, Popocatepetl, the "smoky mountain,"

and Ixtacihuatl, the "recumbent woman."
On the other side of these mountains, the
motorcade entered the delightfully charming
city of Puebla, founded in 1531 as a fortress
to protect Mexico City. Here in this most
Spanish of all Mexican cities, the pope met a
crowd of 80,000 in the city's soccer stadium
and then went on to the Palafoxana Seminary
on the outskirts of town to convene the
Third Latin American Bishops' Conference.

The vast majority of Mexicans
welcomed the pope with wild enthusiasm.
Hundreds of thousands turned out to greet
him wherever he went. In turn, the Holy
Father showed himself overwhelmed by
the piety and faith of the people. Thus,
celebrating Mass in Mexico City's historic
cathedral, the supreme pontiff expressed his
admiration for the country's religious fervor.
Then, in talks to priests, nuns, the Polish
colony in the nation's capital, and the
tremendous crowds at the national shrine of
Our Lady of Guadalupe, he expressed his
special delight at being a pilgrim in the land
whose devotion to the Blessed Virgin was
like that of his native Poland.

Warmth and affection had been evident
as the pope motored to Puebla, standing in a
specially constructed vehicle so that he could
greet the thousands who lined the highway
to see him pass. However, the reaction to his
long, complex speech opening the Puebla
conference was more complicated. He spoke
of the church's involvement with liberating
men from sin and oppression but deliberately
avoided any reference to the "theology of
liberation." He said that in the church's early
tradition, Christ had not been looked upon
as a revolutionary seeking to overthrow a
political order and that politics was principally
the province of the laity. He also remarked
that poverty was not always and necessarily evil
and referred to "the simple joys of the poor."

This speech disturbed not only many
listeners but also others around the world to
whom the pope's words were reported. At the
very least, the Holy Father seemed to be
opposing church involvement in social and
political action. Actually, although many
people failed to see it, the papal message
was a positive statement of the church's
involvement in freeing all mankind of the
shackles of both personal and social evils.

The Holy Father's true feelings and

*The pope receives a good-by
kiss from an admirer as he
prepares to leave Mexico City.*

A beautiful handcrafted floral arrangement delights the pope.

convictions became clearer the next day in a speech he gave to some forty thousand Indian peasants near Oaxaca.

JANUARY 29, 1979:
OAXACA

Oaxaca state and Oaxaca city sit high on a plain surrounded by tall mountains huddled shoulder to shoulder. Founded by the Aztecs in 1486, this lush town's predominant color is green. Like Puebla, it is a typically colonial city. The center of its life is the town square, with its kiosks and *portales,* its iron benches, stately laurel trees, and serenely beautiful flower beds. There are few modern buildings here, and the city reflects its ancient past, its Zapotec and Mixtec Indian heritage, more than the contemporary world.

Oaxaca is a noted marketplace where one can buy various examples of Indian crafts: woven goods, ceramics, leather goods, *rebozos* (woolen shawls), and *serapes* (thick woolen blankets). But Oaxaca is also notorious as one of Mexico's most backward and impoverished areas. It was this poverty that Pope John Paul II was forced by sheer emotion to confront, and he did so humbly

*Framed by majestic cloud-covered
mountains, the papal procession moves
forward in dignity and reverence.*

and with humanity.

This unexpected confrontation came at
the Indian village of Cuilapan de Guerrero,
eight miles outside of Oaxaca city. Wearing
tattered cottons, the descendants of once-
glorious civilizations, whose ruins are now
buried under the jungles of the area, met the
leader of their faith. Mothers carried
undernourished babies wrapped in worn,
frayed shawls. Men stood barefooted,
work and struggle having melted the youth
from their faces, leaving them old before
their time. These Indians, quiet by nature
and solemn by force of habit, were somewhat
overawed by the pope's appearance, surprised
mostly by the helicopter by which he had
come to their village from Oaxaca. They had
tried to learn to say, "Welcome, fisherman,"
in Polish in his honor, but even with the
help of cheerleaders they couldn't quite
make it work. Instead, they waved yellow
and white Vatican flags they had been given.

The pope sat on a huge podium and
watched as groups of Indians performed
ancient dances for him. To his front in the
distance were the ruins of Monte Albán,
a fifth-century Zapotec ceremonial center;
immediately to his right were the ruins of the
once-sumptuous sixteenth-century Dominican
monastery and church that had been
abandoned during the Revolution of 1910.

The pope was obviously moved by what
he saw before him: the immense poverty,
the downtrodden Indians, their faces creased
with hopelessness. Only the children seemed
gay as they flocked around His Holiness,
one enticing him to put on a multicolored
feathered headdress that had been worn
during a performance of the "Dance of the
Feathers," a dance the pope liked so much
he requested an encore and got it.

Then, in a dramatic response to the
misery he had seen, he made an emotional
speech denouncing the injustice of poverty.
"It is not Christian," he said, "to maintain
unjust situations." But he did urge his listeners
to use not violence but, spiritual and moral
persuasion to overcome "unjust situations."

After by far the most moving moment
of his pilgrimage, His Holiness returned to
Oaxaca to say Mass in the city cathedral
and then ordain ten Indians as priests.

*A throng of gaily
beribboned young
girls greets the pope.*

*John Paul II bends to embrace
a young Mexican lad in
sombrero and serape.*

JANUARY 30, 1979:
GUADALAJARA

After spending the night in Mexico
City, the papal party left on a government-
provided jet and flew to Guadalajara,
a sprawling city located several hundred miles
west of Mexico City in the State of Jalisco.

Guadalajara is a city of broad contrasts.
It is divided into four distinct sections, each
with its own culture, atmosphere, and
unique attractions.

Jaliscans love to dance, and they love
the vibrant, highly romantic mariachi
music as accompaniment to that dancing.
Guadalajara, in fact, is where mariachi music
began. So popular is this music here that it
has a plaza of its very own, the Plazuela de
Mariachis. All over the city on any given day
or night, one can see the various Jaliscan
dances performed and hear the jaunty, sadly
humorous, *grito*-punctuated (a *grito* is a
shout similar to an *olé*) mariachi music
in settings reflecting hundreds of years of
various influences, including Spanish, French,
Indian, and *ranchero* (the Mexican cowboy).

Here, before a crowd of several hundred
thousand, Pope John Paul II summed up the
intent of his pilgrimage to Mexico: to bring
Christian attention to the poor and the needy
and to offer them, through the auspices of
his high office, his guidance and spiritual
and moral support in coping with the
injustices of social and economic conditions.
He had come from Rome in order to meet
them, to understand them better, and,
hopefully, to unify them in a common effort
to alleviate the grim problems they face.

The whole day at Guadalajara was
festive, as the pope was entertained by a
Polish orchestra, several children's choirs,
and mariachi and military bands. The human
interaction was so warm that John Paul's
takeoff was two hours behind schedule.
The plane then circled the city for twenty
minutes as a million Guadalajarans below
flashed their farewell by focusing sun-
reflecting mirrors on the plane.

Before returning to Rome, in his last stop
in Mexico, at Monterrey on Tuesday evening,
January 30, the Holy Father again spoke to
thousands of workers and farmers, exhibiting
his understanding of and sympathy for their
plight. Recognizing that many Mexicans feel
they must leave home to find work in other
lands — particularly, the United States — the

The Third Latin American Bishops' Conference at Puebla, Mexico, January 28, 1979.

pontiff said, "We cannot shut our eyes to the plight of those who abandon their homeland in search of employment. . .and often have to live in conditions unworthy of human beings."

On his last stop in America, this time at Nassau in the Bahamas, he delivered a midnight talk to thousands assembled in a local sports stadium.

The papal plane returned to Rome that evening with a very exhausted but happy and satisfied pope taking a much-needed rest on a specially prepared bed built into the plane.

In public statements made directly after leaving the New World, the pope clarified the meaning of his Puebla address, stating that it did not contain a contradiction. Its aim was to inspire the bishops to go forward in the direction indicated by the "Medellin Manifesto." They were to seek "new ways, new frames of mind" to carry out the church's mission, bringing a new consciousness of peace and justice to Latin America.

During the Puebla conference, the Latin American prelates did just that. They produced documents imbued with a positive approach to preaching the Gospel by word and by example. They insisted that the good

news of man's redemption had to be lived on all levels of society. Moreover, they condemned oppression, torture, and exploitation by governments, corporations, greedy landowners, and foreign financial interests, while encouraging their people to gain a new consciousness of their dignity as brothers and sisters in Jesus Christ.

Shortly afterward, in a public audience at the Vatican, Pope John Paul II praised what had been accomplished at Puebla. He formally accepted the "theology of liberation" as a valid expression of the church's teaching of the Gospel.

The Puebla program included a commitment to man's worldly existence as seen under the umbrella of Christ's words and deeds. It demanded liberation from sinfulness of all kinds through Christ's redemption. It stressed the duty of the individual to imitate our Lord in daily actions. It insisted on the obligation of the rich and the powerful to respect the rights of the poor and the oppressed and to cooperate to enable everyone — men, women, and children of every race, color, religion, and socioeconomic level — to live with the dignity that belongs to the sons and daughters of Almighty God.

A month later, in his first encyclical, *Redemptor Hominis (The Redeemer of Man)*, Pope John Paul II confirmed this program as a primary aim of his pontificate.

3

AMONG THE PEOPLE IN ITALY

When John Paul II returned to Rome on February 1, 1979, from his pilgrimage to Mexico, he had become a center of world attention. The trip had been his first overseas visit, among a people overwhelmingly Catholic yet of a different nature and culture than those familiar to him in his native Eastern Europe. Coverage of the trip was thorough, for representatives of the media meant to test this man who had come to the papacy with so many broad-reaching and enthusiastically proclaimed ideals. Many of them just couldn't see how he could live up to these ideals, given the state of the Catholic church and the overall discontent in the world regarding all established institutions.

But John Paul passed the test and emerged from the Mexican trip having accomplished all that had been expected of him and then some. Observers had been tough on him, combing his every action for weaknesses, his every statement for contradictions or faux pas. And there were several tense moments during the trip, mostly revolving around the "theology of liberation" issue at the Puebla conference. But John Paul came out of these ideological and factional storms relatively dry and certainly unperturbed by the strength of the downpours.

Back in Rome, he reassumed his papal duties at the Vatican with even more ardor than before. He had fulfilled the highest expectations: he was a tough political fighter; he was an orator of immense power; he was "pragmatically self-reliant"; his charismatic influence was overwhelming; he was a vigorous leader; he was on top of any issue to which he addressed himself; he seemed able to unify the church and direct it toward new growth and vitality.

His major responsibilities following the Mexican trip were mainly doctrinal in nature: preparing his first encyclical; composing a letter to the priests giving his views on that body's growing discontent over the question of celibacy; organizing his opinions on world events, in particular, on the blight of terrorism, continuing to be so widespread as a revolutionary tactic from Northern Ireland to the Middle East and South America. During the Lenten season, his audiences seemed to involve more people and occupy more of his time every day.

Surrounded by skiers, John Paul II, wearing a white parka, is presented with a medallion.

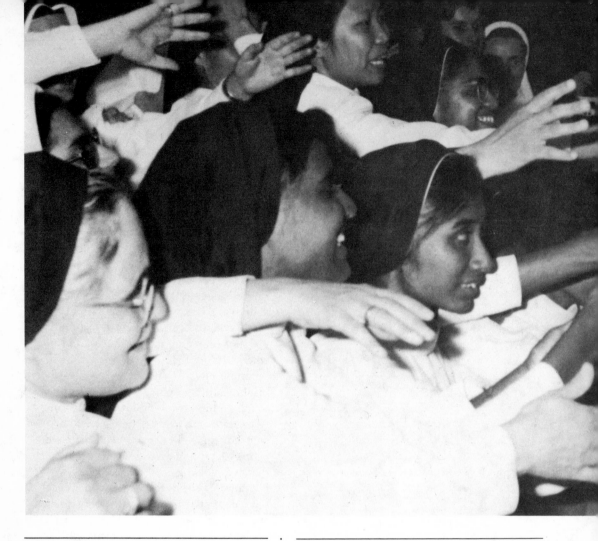

FEBRUARY 21, 1979:
JUSTICE

With the extreme poverty he had seen
in Mexico and the intense concern for it
shown by the prelates of Latin America still
fresh in his mind, His Holiness issued his
strongest statement to date on social justice
and human rights during a press conference
in Rome on February 21, 1979.

In this statement, John Paul built the
foundation on which he would stand when
confronted by the issue in the future.
He deplored placing economic, technological,
and political millstones around the necks of
people, rendering men, women, and children
slaves to systems and institutions instead of
the other way around. "We must declare by
name," he stated, "every violence committed
against man's body, against his spirit,
his conscience, and his conviction." He stated
his allegiance to the poor of the world,
to taking up their cause and fighting for
their liberation from injustice. From now on,
his pilgrimages would express that cause.

FEBRUARY 25, 1979:
THE MARRIAGE OF
VITTORIA IANNI AND MARIO MALTESE

Earlier in the year, while he was visiting
among the people touring the Vatican —
surprise appearances he is apt to make on the
spur of the moment — a young woman who
just happened to meet His Holiness asked,
couching her question with lighthearted half-
seriousness, if he would perform her marriage
ceremony. To her amazement, he agreed.
On February 25, under the Michelangelo
frescoes in the Vatican Palace, John Paul
performed the nuptial Mass for Vittoria
Ianni, twenty-two, the daughter of a Rome
street cleaner, and Mario Maltese, twenty-
four, a young electrician. As gifts, the pope
presented the couple with a leather-bound
Bible, a picture of the Virgin Mary, and an
unspecified amount of money. Then the
pope, to the excitement of everyone, kissed
the bride. He was again given occasion to
emphasize his views on marriage and the
family and his firm objection to divorce.

Nuns eagerly reach out to touch the hands of Pope John Paul II.

MARCH 16, 1979:
REDEMPTOR HOMINIS

On March 16, an event that attracted less publicity than the Mexican trip but was more significant in the long run took place. It was the publication of Pope John Paul II's first encyclical, a twenty-four-thousand-word statement entitled *Redemptor Hominis (The Redeemer of Man).*

In this document, the pope set down his position on church policies, his views on world affairs, his intentions for the church, and the focal points of his papal ministry. The encyclical called, first of all, for attention to the welfare of the world's people, for respect for human rights and the sanctity of human life. It deplored inequality based on economic and social injustices and emphasized the need to preserve the earth's resources and to control technology.

The document supported the ecumenical movement and reemphasized John Paul's willingness to share jointly with his bishops the rule of the church. The Holy Father further declared that his papal mission is to take the truth of the Gospel to mankind by going into the world to preach it, just as Jesus taught his disciples to do.

In social, economic, and political terms, the encyclical was boldly liberal, yet regarding internal church matters it was strangely conservative. The pope showed that he was firmly opposed to wide differences of opinion or lack of discipline inside the church with respect to doctrine and practice, though he stressed the need for people to form their own spiritual consciousness. He also came out against innovations in celebrating the Eucharist.

The pope had taken his position on many key issues. It was down in writing. He meant to follow firmly in the footsteps of Christ, calling attention less to the church's political position than to Christ and human needs, the "relation between Christ's redemption and human dignity." Though remaining thoroughly disciplined in its internal makeup, the church under John Paul II was headed in a new direction universally. His emphasis was on the catholic meaning of the church—on making it truly the church of all people.

to the teachings of Christ and to Christian service, remaining, in doing so, free from the contamination and condemnation of sin.

APRIL 9, 1979:
THE STATEMENT ON CELIBACY

Among the critics of the encyclical were a group of priests who read in its remarks about the priesthood a rejection of movements aimed at modifying the Latin church's intransigent stand demanding a celibate clergy. They had hoped that John Paul would at least follow the line of Paul VI, and gradually introduce the option of marriage for the clergy. They had suggested that he allow the priests who had returned to the lay state to function as priests by saying Mass and giving the sacraments. The encyclical contained no such indication. Hence, they appealed to the new pope for a reconsideration. The pope's letter to the priests was his response. It was written spontaneously for the church's celebration of the Last Supper on Holy Thursday, when Jesus Christ ordained the apostles as the first priests. It is, consequently, an exhortation to holiness and deep spiritual awareness rather than a theological statement. But John Paul did take the occasion to reaffirm his total commitment to celibacy for the priests of the Latin church. In so doing, he almost seemed to downgrade the married clergy of the Oriental Catholic churches whose customs go back to the primitive church in which most of the bishops and priests were married.

John Paul further questioned the process for letting priests return to the lay state and let it be known that he was holding up all such requests for further study. He seemed to ignore the agony of priests who had left the ministry and now wanted to solve their conscience problems, particularly after his predecessor, Paul VI, who was scrupulous about such matters, had given such dispensations. While welcomed by the majority of conservative faithful, John Paul's letter to his priests caused great anguish among those looking for an authentic, updated renewal of the church promised by the new Holy Father.

Celibacy, he stated, is in respect of the purity and perfection Christ exemplified while here on earth. The priest, as an emissary of Christ, must sacrifice his whole body and mind

THE CHURCH AND THE WORLD

After his return from Mexico, John Paul found that he could look with new insight at problems facing the church all over the globe. During the Mexican interlude, he had become fully conscious of the "church of confessors and martyrs," Christians' faith in action for justice in many of the Latin American countries, whose bishops he had encountered at Puebla. Although he said that Christ was not a revolutionary, the Holy Father began to realize that he himself was considered subversive by many of the rich and powerful. After all, he had called for a rethinking of government policies in these lands, demanding the elimination of unjust economic and social patterns and insisting on human rights and human dignity.

As he glanced at the map of Africa, he realized the great grief and destruction the church was suffering in the newly liberated lands of that continent. From Chad and Uganda in the north to Namibia and South Africa in the south, mission stations, schools, parishes, and community centers were victims of marauding guerrillas or irresponsible government officials.

Nevertheless, in all these countries, the church was actually flourishing. Thousands of new Christians were being baptized each week, while hundreds of young men and women were being instructed as catechists and teachers or experiencing the call to the religious life and Holy Orders. Indeed, the African church was not only surviving under grave pressures but was also showing the world that Catholicism is every bit as vital there as it is elsewhere in the world.

In the Middle East, people of several faiths were suffering the effects of war in countries like Lebanon, Ethiopia, and Iran. Meanwhile, no resolution was in sight for the explosive situation involving the Israelis, the Palestinians, and the Arab world. Pope John Paul II made it clear to leaders on all sides that he was willing to do whatever he could to assist movements for peace. (He provided this assistance in another part

To this little girl, despite his smile and soothing words, the pope is just a stranger.

of the globe when he sent Antonio Cardinal Samore at the request of Argentina and Chile to help arbitrate a territorial dispute between the two countries.)

Gazing at the map of Asia, the pope saw grave danger spots for both mankind and the Catholic church. Yet he also saw reasons for hope. Though harassed by anti-Christian laws in India and Sri Lanka, the church was doing better than holding its own. And as the Holy Father reflected on the horrors being inflicted on Southeast Asia, including the forced exile of the so-called "boat people," he could still take heart from the way the church was regearing itself to cope with the demands of new Communist regimes. At the Roman Synod of Bishops in 1977, the archbishop of Ho Chi Minh City (formerly Saigon) had assured Pope Paul VI that the church would adapt itself to the new order in Southeast Asia as it once had adapted itself to the repressive Roman Empire in which it saw the light of day.

Furthermore, there were indications that the church in the People's Republic of China was still alive despite the purges of the Mao Tse-tung regime and the xenophobic upheavals of the 1966 revolution. In fact, Rome received word that Chinese priests who wanted to visit their homeland would be welcomed, and a large number of exiles traveled to their native towns and villages, slowly discovering priests and bishops who were still functioning underground.

The Chinese authorities even indicated willingness to allow the Jesuits to reopen their medical college, the Aurora, in Shanghai. At the same time, however, they wanted reorganization of the Patriotic Catholic Association, which had kept the church together during the thirty years of Communist rule. Pope John Paul II would have much praying to do before making up his mind about how to resolve the situation.

He would also have to pray over the church in the Philippines, where President and Mrs. Ferdinand E. Marcos, using their ostensibly Catholic government, were obviously oppressing the people by gathering land and wealth into the hands of their family and friends and persecuting priests, nuns, and bishops who demanded justice and Christian dignity for the people.

In Indonesia, the church was sustaining both great gains and tough losses. Catholics in Japan, though but a handful, were well respected with an excellent hierarchy. John Paul acknowledged this fact by making the archbishop of Nagasaki a cardinal. In troubled South Korea, the church was on the side of dignity and justice. In the South Pacific, on the great Australian continent and New Zealand, the church, however, was able to pursue its mission in comparative peace.

Peace was not the word for church affairs in Western Europe, however, which the pope well realized as he contemplated the situation in the Netherlands. Catholics there represented 40 percent of the population, and a large proportion attended Sunday Mass and received the sacraments. But many priests, nuns, and lay people wanted radical changes on moral and doctrinal issues, including sex and marriage, clerical celibacy, liturgy and the sacraments, and Catholic school teaching. On the other hand, there was strong opposition to these changes among many of the Dutch clergy and laity.

After a number of conferences, the Dutch bishops agreed to disagree and appealed to Rome. John Paul II called them to the Vatican one by one, listened to their ideas, and finally advised them to prepare for a synod under his scrutiny in Rome. The pope was playing for time and divine inspiration, for the Dutch church's solutions to these disputes might help him deal with similar problems in other countries of Europe and the rest of the world.

In France, although there were signs of a revival of faith, the church on the whole lacked its former vigor. Vocations to the priesthood were down, the religious orders were having a difficult time finding recruits, and there was considerable agitation for a married priesthood, in particular, acceptance by Rome of priests who left the church to marry.

There were also problems created by specific French churchmen. One, the arch-conservative French bishop, Marcel Lefebvre, had denounced changes in the church's teaching and liturgy and attracted many followers with his own traditionalist doctrines and liturgy sacraments. He continued to say Mass, confirm children, and ordain priests even though his right to say Mass and confer the sacraments had been suspended by Pope Paul VI. Then a French Dominican, Jacques Pohier, wrote a book entitled *When I Say God*, which John Paul II found so objectionable that he condemned it in Rome by name, something very rare since the Vatican II Council.

In Spain and Portugal, the church was recuperating from the Franco and Salazár dictatorships. In Portugal, there were almost a million former residents of Angola and Mozambique, many of whom had lost everything when expelled from these former African colonies. They blamed the church for having supported oppressive Portuguese

Pope John Paul II

...and some of the 566,686,000 people he serves.

policy in these colonies, thus contributing to the bitterness that led to their current plight.

Whatever had been the case in the past, however, church leaders in Spain and Portugal no longer supported or desired repressive right-wing regimes. Instead, they encouraged the formation of democratic governments with constitutions that did not try to give the church any special privileges. Some arch-conservatives opposed this trend and appealed to the pope for support. They did not receive it.

These instances and events in Italy, closer to the Vatican, clearly revealed Pope John Paul II's enlightened and progressive view of what church-state relations should be. Thus, he moved to pull the church back from its traditional involvement in Italian politics and away from Italy's current political troubles. He made it clear that he, as bishop of Rome, would speak out about moral issues and values in Italian life but that it was up to the bishops themselves to decide how they would guide, not dominate, the Italian voter. As a result of this move, many Catholics who had been voting for the left in protest against Vatican political influence have apparently begun to return to the Christian Democrat party, with consequent loss of support by the Communists.

As John Paul considered church activities in Western Europe as a whole, he found a vigorous effort being made by bishops, priests, and lay leaders to regain the interest and loyalty of youth, a movement close to the pope's heart. Each Wednesday before the general audience, he began holding a special audience in Saint Peter's for young people from all over the world. In these meetings, he displayed his great gift for penetrating the psychology of young people. At the same time, with bishops and statemen, he has displayed troubled concern with one of Europe's and the world's main problems, lack of meaningful work for everyone, but especially for young people.

In the months after his return from Mexico, Pope John Paul II had many problems and opportunities to reflect and act upon — not only those discussed above but those in other areas of the world as well. He had shown himself to be conservative in doctrinal and moral matters but forward looking and liberal regarding social, economic, and political questions. His warm personality, powerful figure, and openness in dealing with people had earned him great popularity throughout the world.

Naturally, observers looked forward to the pope's trip to Poland, his native land, with great interest and also, perhaps, with apprehension. After his election, John Paul chose to continue the policy of Paul VI toward Eastern Europe, seeking détente and even cooperation with the Communist regimes there. On the other hand, Karol Wojtyla had never been one to brook interference by political authorities with the mission of the church. At the very least, the pilgrimage to Poland promised to produce moments of high drama and to reveal new dimensions of this remarkable new pope's character and personality.

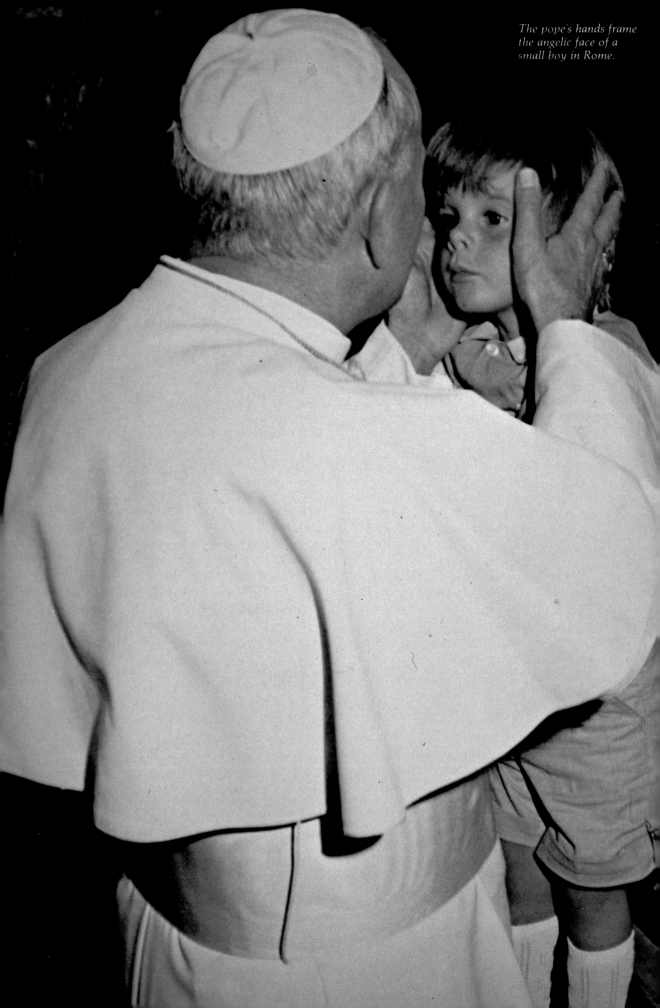

The pope's hands frame the angelic face of a small boy in Rome.

The pope with Mr. and
Mrs. Mario Maltese.

4
RETURN TO POLAND

What could be more fitting for the first Polish pope than a pilgrimage to his native land in order to celebrate the martyrdom of Saint Stanislaus, Poland's patron saint? Other popes had been invited to Poland, notably by the archbishop of Krakow, Karol Cardinal Wojtyla, who had asked both Pope Paul VI and Pope John Paul I to visit his country. Unfortunately, in both cases, death intervened to prevent the trip. When Karol Wojtyla himself became pope, however, Stefan Cardinal Wyszynski, the leader of the Polish Catholic church, recommended that he himself accept the invitation. By so doing, he would give the Polish people the opportunity to venerate one of their own who had become the supreme pontiff of the Roman Catholic church.

Pope John Paul II accepted the invitation, and plans for the trip were put into motion. This required negotiations between church authorities and representatives of the People's Republic of Poland and its Communist party. The government demanded that the trip be purely spiritual, with no political overtones, and reserved the right to specify where the pope could and could not visit. Moreover, there was a conflict over the date of the trip. The Polish authorities refused to allow the visit to coincide with May 8, the traditional date of the martyrdom of Saint Stanislaus, proposing instead that it be postponed until June. The church had no choice but to agree, whereupon the cardinal primate declared the celebration a "movable feast" and shifted it to early June.

The government's qualms about the trip were not without justification. Ninety percent of the 35 million Poles are practicing Catholics. The church represents a link to past tradition for older people and a viable opposition to the Communist party for dissident young people. At the moment of the trip, economic problems were creating unrest in most Polish Catholics.

Nevertheless, a Communist official stated that meetings about the trip between representatives of church and state had been marked by "cordiality." In that atmosphere of cordiality, the first visit ever by a pope to a Communist country was set to begin. The most famous Pole of all was returning to his native land.

The pope arrives in his hometown, Wadowice.

The pope reviews the guard at the airport.

The pope in the midst of a cheering crowd

JUNE 2–3, 1979: WARSAW

At 10:00 A.M., on June 2, 1979, the white Boeing 727 carrying Pope John Paul II from Rome to Warsaw touched down at Okecie Airport. At 10:17 A.M., the pope, followed by his entourage, descended to touch Polish soil for the first time since he had attained his high office. In a move that was not on the agenda, His Holiness knelt on the airport's tarmac to kiss the ground of Poland.

After the greeting at the airport, the pilgrimage began by moving slowly, in chaotic splendor, toward central Warsaw. The crowds along the way, estimated in the millions, were jubilant and smiling. They tossed flowers, flaunted illegal banners proclaiming adulation, and sang the praises of a true national hero.

The motorcade halted in the Old Town Square at the Cathedral of Saint John, where the pope was welcomed by Cardinal Wyszynski. The ceremony was followed by a visit with the Polish primate in his quarters alongside the cathedral.

The papal party then drove to Belvedere Palace, where they were officially welcomed by Edward Gierek, first secretary of the Polish Communist party, President Henryk Jablonski, and other civil authorities.

Upon leaving the palace, the pope moved past tightly compressed crowds lining the streets into Victory Square, where 290,000 people had gathered to see him. A carnival atmosphere reigned as the people sang religious and national songs despite orders to the contrary from a police loudspeaker truck. When the pope arrived, the gaiety and music gave way to sounds of joy as thousands openly wept in happiness and gratitude. After ascending the huge altar constructed at one end of the square, His Holiness celebrated the Eucharist facing the tomb of the unknown soldier. It was the largest single religious observance — and the first papal Mass — ever in a Communist country.

In his homily, he referred to himself as a "pilgrim pope" and emphasized that "Christ cannot be kept out of the history of man in any part of the globe."

The next day, June 3, was Pentecost Sunday, and the pope conducted his second pontifical Mass in Poland outside Saint Anne's Church in Castle Square, in the university district of Warsaw. Here he spoke

Meeting in the baroque Basilica of the Shrine of Jasna Gora

The Monastery of Jasna Gora

to some 250,000 youths, many of them students. His appeal to the young was an important part of his mission, for it is the young who keep the Polish church forward looking, and their respect for it is based primarily on its refusal to bow to the state.

JUNE 3, 1979: GNIEZNO

On the afternoon of June 3, the pope arrived by helicopter (a mode of transportation he openly found thrilling) at Gniezno, Poland's primatial see, to be greeted by 10,000 people gathered in a meadow outside of town. From there the papal procession made its way to the historic Cathedral of the Archdiocese of Gniezno, past crowds less self-restrained than those in Warsaw. The pope relished every minute of it, acting more jovially than ever, kissing babies, shaking hands, and joining in songs.

During the homily given in honor of Pentecost at the cathedral, His Holiness noticed a sign held by a Czech group; it said, "Father, remember your Czech church." The pope interrupted his discourse to acknowledge the message on the sign, stating that he was the pope of the Slavs and that he would not forget those of his faith throughout Eastern Europe.

JUNE 4–6, 1979: CZESTOCHOWA

On the morning of June 4, Pope John Paul II came by helicopter from Gniezno to Czestochowa, a city of 200,000 in southern Poland. Here 500,000 waited to see him pass en route to the Monastery of Jasna Gora "bright mountain." Here is located the famed shrine of Our Lady of Czestochowa, an ancient icon painted on wood depicting the Holy Mother holding the baby Jesus on her lap. Colloquially called "the Black Madonna" because of its dark coloring, it is one of the most valuable and widely revered treasures of the Polish nation.

At noon, the pope celebrated a three-hour Mass from the ramparts of the monastery during which the large audience fell to its knees in unison as His Holiness elevated the host and consecrated himself and the entire church to Mary.

The pope speaking at
Saint Mary's Church
in Krakow

Then, alone and in deep earnestness, he entered the monastery to pray, kneeling motionless in his white cassock at the feet of the Black Madonna.

On the second day of his stay in Czestochowa, the pope addressed the Polish Bishops' Conference, convened that week to coincide with his visit. He talked of the "normalization" of church-state relations in Poland. The tone of his speeches, homilies, and papers was becoming stronger, more sharply political now, particularly in his challenges to the government to "respect the cause of fundamental human rights, including the right to religious liberty."

By the end of his meeting with the bishops, thousands of pilgrims from Lower Silesia had gathered on the slopes of Jasna Gora to attend another of the pope's outdoor Masses. They included a contingent of coal miners wearing the colorful, century-old ceremonial uniform of miners of that region. On their chests were rows of crosses, medallions, and "leading worker" badges.

"Work," the pope said to them, "is the fundamental dimension of man's existence. Work has for man a significance that is not merely technical but ethical." He also had these words for all who work: "Do not let yourselves be seduced by the temptation to think that man can fully find himself by denying God, erasing prayer from his life, and remaining only a worker, deluding himself with believing that what he produces can on its own fill the needs of the human heart."

JUNE 6, 1979:
KRAKOW

When the helicopter brought Pope John Paul II from Czestochowa to Krakow on June 6, half a million spectators were there to meet him. The pope, wearing a crimson cloak over his white vestments, was astonished by the reception.

But Krakow could have been expected to give him an extraordinary reception, for it was in this city of 500,000 that Karol Wojtyla served as bishop, archbishop, and cardinal, coming there at the beginning of World War II when he was active in the resistance movement against the Nazi occupation.

"Krakow," the pope said in homage to this great city upon his arrival, "from the tenderest years of my life, has been for me a particular synthesis of all that it means to be Polish and Catholic."

On the night of June 6, His Holiness went to his old apartment in the archbishop's palace on Franciszkanska Street to rest and sleep, but a crowd gathered below in the street, encouraging the pope to appear at one of the windows. Eager to get closer to the people, he hopped on to the windowsill, with unidentified hands holding on to his cassock to ensure his safety.

He talked and even sang with the crowd of well-wishers until midnight when, obviously fatigued but still jubilant, he got in the last word: "You are asking for a word or two," he said, "so here they are: Good night!"

JUNE 7, 1979:
HOMECOMING TO WADOWICE

Forty miles south of Krakow, near the Czechoslovakian border, lies the complex of churches known as Kalwaria Zebrzydowska, the site of the shrine of the Holy Mother of Kalwaria. His Holiness arrived here on the morning of June 7 to offer prayers at the foot of the shrine. He had been coming to

Hundreds of thousands attended the pontifical Mass at Birkenau.

the shrine since his boyhood in Wadowice some ten kilometers away.

A helicopter then carried the pontiff from Kalwaria to his home town for a two-hour visit, landing in a stadium outside of town. A limousine brought Pope John Paul II into the square of the village where he was born, baptized, and educated as a Catholic.

A principal market center for a large farming district, Wadowice, with a population of 15,000, is a green, clean country village. The outstanding structure on the town square is the church, freshly painted a bright yellow and white in preparation for the return of the village's most famous son. His Holiness entered the church and, in a small side chapel so familiar to him, prayed before a picture of Our Lady of Perpetual Help, just as he had done so many times when he was a teenager and later as a young priest and then bishop, archbishop, and cardinal.

Across the street from the church, newly cut flowers surrounded the base of the baptismal font in which, in 1920, Karol Wojtyla was christened and received into the Catholic family.

At the end of his visit, standing on the church steps, the pope saluted the people jammed into the village square, throwing away his prepared text to chat convivially with them, leading and joining them in hymns and "Polonia Semper Fidelis" to the accompaniment of the Wadowice village orchestra.

JUNE 7, 1979:
AUSCHWITZ-BIRKENAU

The papal party left Wadowice by helicopter at 2:00 P.M., whirling its way westward a few miles to what during World War II had been known as Konzentrationslager Auschwitz-Birkenau, a place in which 4 million defenseless human beings were systematically and routinely put to death, over 2 million of them simply because they were Jewish. His Holiness called this visit "a pilgrimage to the heart of cruelty and hatred."

Inside the main camp at Auschwitz, His Holiness walked along a fence of concrete poles connected by barbed wire to what is called the Wall of Death. Against the wall, more than 20,000 inmates were shot by the Nazis.

At the foot of the wall, the pope placed a wreath, then knelt a moment in silent prayer.

A helicopter then transported the pope to Birkenau (also known as Auschwitz II), two and a half miles away. Here was the main extermination center as well as the crematoria of the whole Auschwitz complex.

Here the pope celebrated Mass on an altar constructed of wood from the railroad platform where those selected "for gassing" arrived at the camp. Over the altar was a cross "haloed" by a crown of thorns.

In his homily, the pope called the place "this Golgotha of the modern world" and, quoting Pope Paul VI's address to the United Nations in 1965, called for "no more war, war never again. It is peace, peace which must guide the destinies of peoples and of all mankind."

It was a long, difficult Mass, and toward the end it became evident that the exertions demanded by the prodigious trip were affecting the pope's health. Indeed, the next day it was announced that he was suffering from a "low-grade infection" of the throat.

The snow-covered Tatra Mountains

JUNE 8, 1979:
NOWY TARG AND
A RETURN TO KRAKOW

After the solemn, traumatic, and humbling experience of Auschwitz, the pope returned to Krakow for a night of rest. The next day, June 8, he flew southwest to Nowy Targ, high up in the snow-covered and cloud-shrouded Tatra Mountains. Among these mountains a younger Karol Wojtyla had spent many hours, days, and months in hiking, camping, and skiing.

The reception at Nowy Targ was the most colorful yet, as the highlanders arrived wearing their traditional costumes. Some of them, ignoring the heat, came dressed in the fancy woolen topcoats and sheepskin hats of the mountain area.

In his homily during the Mass he celebrated for these highland people, who have always been dear to his heart, the pope spoke of "the great and fundamental rights of man: the right to work and the right to land."

From Nowy Targ, His Holiness returned to Krakow for the final days of his Polish pilgrimage. Thus, on the afternoon of June 8, he was present in Wawel Cathedral for the closing of the seven-year synod of the Krakow archdiocese, begun in 1972 by the pope when he was the cardinal-archbishop there.

That night, he went to the Skalka Pauline fathers' monastery to speak to some 65,000 university students. "Allow Christ to find you," he exhorted them, adding, "There will be no better world unless preference is first given to the values of the human spirit."

JUNE 9, 1979:
NOWA HUTA

On June 9, His Holiness was to have held services in Nowa Huta, the start-from-scratch industrial city erected near Krakow as an example of socialist planning. The Nowa Huta church was of supreme importance to this pilgrimage because its existence is due almost entirely to Karol Wojtyla. The people wanted it, but the government opposed it. Cardinal Wojtyla, therefore, had to fight for years for permission to build the church. Now it stands, a memorial to his untiring devotion to its cause, and its daring, beautiful modern architecture reflects his forward thinking.

Despite all this — or, perhaps, because

The Nowa Huta Church of the Mother of God

The pope mixing with the crowd in Krakow.

Wawel Cathedral

of it — the Polish goverment would not allow him to visit the church or even the city in which it was located. Since the pope could not go to Nowa Huta, Nowa Huta came to the pope, in the adjacent suburb of Mogila.

In his message to the tens of thousands gathered before him, Pope John Paul II made his harshest political comments of the trip against the regime. "Christ will never approve," he said, "that man be considered, or that man consider himself merely as a means for production, or that he be appreciated, esteemed, and valued in accordance with that principle."

Returning to Krakow, the pope spent the remainder of the day, first, visiting the graves of his parents and brother at Kakowiecki Cemetery; second, meeting with monks and nuns at Saint Mary's church, near the cemetery; and third, meeting with the sick and lame at a large Franciscan church, which also offered him a concert of sacred music.

He rested that night, the last he would spend in Poland on this trip, in the archbishop's residence at the Wawel Cathedral.

JUNE 10, 1979:
SAINT STANISLAUS—AND FAREWELL

The ninth and last day of Pope John Paul II's trip was, appropriately enough, devoted to celebrating the 900th anniversary of the martyrdom of Saint Stanislaus. In 1079, Poland's patron saint was stoned to death for opposing, as bishop of Krakow, the tyrannical regime that ruled his land. In 1979, the Polish government reportedly prevented the pope from coming home on or near May 8, the day on which, for centuries, Poles have celebrated their martyred patron saint. However, even though formal ceremonies were conducted on the traditional May date, for most Poles the real 900th anniversary celebration occurred on Sunday, June 10, 1979, the day the pope knelt in front of the gold-canopied altar wherein lie the remains of the beloved saint.

The high, pontifical Mass in honor of Saint Stanislaus was held at the Blonie parade grounds in Krakow. More than a million people, the largest crowd of the trip, were present.

The words of the pope's inspiring Saint Stanislaus homily reached emotional heights as, with voice trembling with feeling and fervor, he said, "And so, before I leave you, I wish to give one more look at Krakow, this Krakow, in which every stone and every brick is dear to me. And I look once more on my Poland." He then ended by begging his fellow Poles to keep the faith in their spiritual legacy and to always hold fast to what this spirituality has given them.

After the Mass, he returned to his temporary residence in his old cathedral apartment, riding past massive, warm crowds that knew that this man, this Pole, carries within him the same indomitable Polish spirit they possess.

It was now time for the pope to say farewell to his homeland. A long motorcade wound through the streets of Krakow, again jammed with admiring well-wishers, and headed to the airport for the departure ceremony.

After a speech by President Jablonski, Cardinal Wyszynski bade his farewell. "You comforted our hearts," he said to his visibly moved friend and pope, whose head was bowed as if he were doing all he could to fight back tears, "with your living belief."

Pope John Paul II then said his good-bye. "It is necessary that I return to Rome, where no son of the church . . . no man, Pole or son of any other nation, is a stranger. I wish you all the best: successes, implementation of your noble plans, and rightful struggles in all domains of life."

Then His Holiness, after kneeling and kissing the ground, entered the airliner that would take him back to the Eternal City.

THE MEANING OF
THE PILGRIMAGE TO POLAND

John Paul II's nine-day visit to Poland included a series of extraordinary events that showed the Polish people — and the world — the optimistic side of the Christian religion.

Celebrating Mass in the public squares of Warsaw, Gniezno, Krakow, and at the former concentration camp of Birkenau before hundreds of thousands of people, the Holy Father exemplified a sense of the splendor of the church. This world leader, who took over the papacy at the moment when, in the political order, there was no one of great stature, gave witness to Christ's presence in the world as well as in the hearts of believers in a very special way.

The message John Paul preached and demonstrated by his actions is that human life is not merely precious. It possesses an internal dignity that no one in state or church has a right to impede for any reason. That dignity consists in the right and ability of every man, woman, and child to feel at home with God by practicing his or her religion freely and publicly and by carrying out the duties involved in religious belief by loving one's neighbor as oneself.

This was the burden of all of John Paul's talks and activities in Poland, from his official meeting with the first secretary of the Communist party, Edward Gierek, in the Belvedere Palace, to his short stopover at the house where he was born and the church in which he was baptized in Wadowice.

In all he did, John Paul presented the Communist authorities and the Marxist ideology with a direct and absolute challenge. Without attacking the drabness of the atheistic creed preached by the Polish ideologists, the Holy Father pointed to the fact that Christianity was not a religion that promised "pie in the sky!" It was an immediate commitment to the well-being of every man, woman, and child born into the world. More than that, it preached a message of the essential goodness lodged in mankind.

Some time before departing Rome for Warsaw, John Paul had published his first encyclical letter, *Redemptor Hominis (The Redeemer of Man)*. It was a long, complicated meditation on the human race and its presence in the universe. A stream-of-consciousness analysis of man's sinfulness, which the pope called "the futility of creation," the document stressed the fact that all of mankind, from the first man and woman, Adam and Eve, down to the last individual to be conceived before the end of time, was already redeemed in Jesus Christ's death and resurrection. *The Redeemer of Man* insisted that as God's creation, endowed with human dignity, though flawed with the ability to do wrong, every individual human being enjoyed God's grace and love. What was more, in the life of every man, woman, and child, Jesus Christ was the focal point and the final end of history.

This startling contention was the basis of the pope's message everywhere he went. Talking to the Polish youth, both the workers and the university students, John Paul told them that without Jesus Christ in their lives they had no way of rising above the material achievements of the twentieth century — all of which could disappear with a major catastrophe. He told the townspeople and older citizens that without Jesus Christ their lives would be an empty struggle for food, clothing, and a few worldly possessions, with no significant meaning. And he told the people assembled at Auschwitz that without Jesus Christ in their hearts, men and women could be guilty of the most incredible crimes against their fellow human beings — a fact attested to so starkly by this modern "Golgotha."

As observers and political commentators attempted to assess what the pope's visit to Poland had achieved, most were at a loss. They recognized his ability to turn out the multitudes — not necessarily a personal gift but a result of the circumstances of his Polish origin and the opportunity he supplied for the people to show the government where their loyalities were lodged. They applauded his fearlessness in challenging the Communist authorities to grant the church the full religious freedom required by the state's constitution. And they envied his ability to reach out over the barriers of national boundaries to comfort the peoples prevented by their governments from coming to see or even only hear the Polish Holy Father.

All these accomplishments were in keeping with the strange phenomenon of a pope — as he said so often himself, a Slav — having the freedom to travel and preach behind the Iron Curtain. But what the outside world and the pope himself wanted to know was: did his visit mean that the majority of the Polish people, and particularly the younger generation, would dig in and deepen their religious practice and commitment to Jesus Christ? And, if they did so without attempting to use direct political means, how long would it take before their rejection of the Communist creed would have an effect on the government?

There could be no doubt that within the Kremlin as well as in the inner circle of the Polish party, grave questions were being asked about the effectiveness of the present party line and how long Russia could afford to keep its expensive military presence in all these countries. But even more important questions were being raised about adopting a new approach to religious practice, with the possibility that it might be used by the state without denying the basic Communist ideology.

Fears that, under Soviet pressure, there would be an attempt to renew a subtle persecution of the church in Poland seemed unwarranted. Before leaving for Puebla, Mexico, in January, John Paul had had a long conversation in the Vatican with Andrei Gromyko, the Russian foreign minister, in which, presumably, understandings had been reached. Nor did predictions that the pope's presence in Poland would be the occasion for political unrest and possible uprisings prove correct.

The pontifical Mass at Birkenau

A realistic political sense, possessed by the pope as well as by the church's lay leaders, recognized the impossibility of outreaching the well-hidden but ever-present cohorts of Soviet military might in all that territory.

What was possible was a change of heart or at least of politics on the part of the more perspicacious of the nation's leaders now that they had experienced a man whose sincerity in his religious beliefs so obviously matched his intelligence and knowledge of the world. After all, the Polish nation had been converted from paganism by the witness of great religious leaders in the past, just as the Roman Empire and the Western world were Christianized by the successors of the apostles.

In a sense, the meaning of Pope John Paul II's tumultuous return to the land of his birth and his penetration of the Iron Curtain as the first Holy Father ever to tread on Slavic soil was fully obvious to the great mass of the Polish people and the world at large. The political leaders of Eastern Europe understood it, too, at least in part. Thus, one party leader in Poland told a Western journalist that after the pope's visit, "thirty years of indoctrination in atheistic ideals would have to be begun all over again." Perhaps, although he might not admit it, the visit also taught him that such "indoctrination" will not, cannot, succeed.

Primate Wyszynski, Pope John Paul II, and President Henryk Jablonski at the farewell ceremonies in Krakow

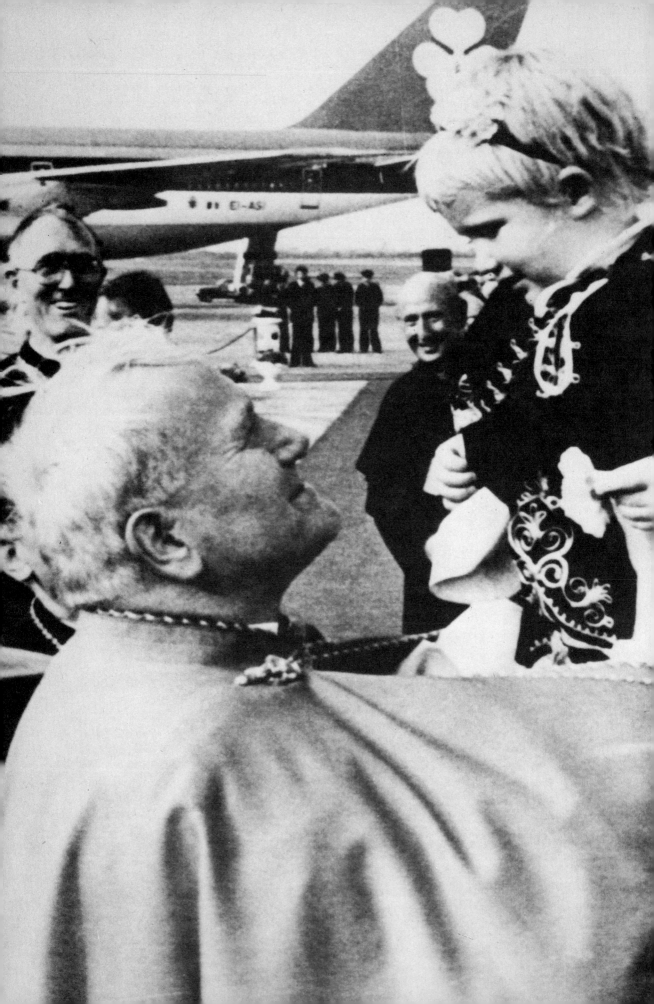

PILGRIMAGE FOR PEACE— IRELAND

5

THE POPE GOES TO IRELAND TO SPREAD A MESSAGE OF PEACE AND BROTHERHOOD

One of the questions put to John Paul II during his first news conference after his election was "Will you come to Ireland?" He replied, "Yes, if they let me!" Among the pope's immediate aides was a youthful Irish priest, John Magee, who had served as John Paul I's private secretary. The very presence of this Gael on the papal staff was a constant reminder to the pope that someday, and soon, he should fulfill his promise.

Of much greater significance, of course, was the commitment he had made in the spring of 1979 to Kurt Waldheim, secretary-general of the United Nations, to visit the General Assembly in New York City, probably on October 4, the fourteenth anniversary of Pope Paul VI's famous speech before that cosmopolitan body. Later, it was decided that Tuesday, October 2, would be a much more auspicious date, for it would allow all the representatives of the 130 member nations the opportunity to welcome the Holy Father.

Irish bishops and civic leaders immediately saw their opportunity. On his way to New York, why couldn't the pope stop over in Ireland, a stop that seemed sensible from both a geographical and a pastoral viewpoint. After considerable negotiation and planning, John Paul decided to make a pastoral visit to the so-called island of saints and scholars from Saturday, September 29, through the morning of Monday, October 1. Among the areas scheduled to be visited was the ancient archdiocese of Armagh in Northern Ireland, whose archbishop, Tomás O'Fiaich, John Paul II had made a cardinal in June. The hope was that a papal visit to Northern Ireland — the scene of so much violence by both the Catholic and Protestant terrorists — would bring a lasting peace.

Instead, the announcement that the pope was going to Ireland occasioned an immediate outcry. Ian Paisley, a Presbyterian minister and a member of the British Parliament, said unhesitatingly, "The pope will not be welcomed in Northern Ireland — a papal visit is not thinkable." In the midst of this clamor came the horrible assassination of the seventy-nine-year-old war hero, the highly esteemed Lord Louis

John Paul lifts up a little girl welcoming him at the Dublin airport

Mountbatten, when his fishing yacht blew up off a seaside resort in southern Ireland, and the fatal attack on eighteen British soldiers by the IRA. These incidents caused such reaction and concern that Pope John Paul was asked by the British government not to set foot in the north. Yielding to both practical concern and the advice of his well-informed counselors, the Holy Father decided not to go to Armagh.

Over 2,000 people have been killed in the last decade in Northern Ireland. Comprised of six counties, it is often called Ulster, and its capital is Belfast. One and a half million people inhabit Ulster; one million are Protestant and want British rule to continue; the remaining half million are Catholic and some favor union with the Republic of Ireland. The contenders in the open hostility afflicting Northern Ireland are two extremist groups: on the one hand, the Irish Republican Army (IRA) and its strike force, the Provisional Irish Republican Army (more popularly known as the Provos), committed to ending British rule; on the other, the staunchly Protestant United Ulster Unionist party, with its terrorist branches, the Ulster Defense Association, and the Ulster Freedom Fighters.

For centuries, Northern Ireland has been a hotbed of sectarian dispute. The Protestants dominate economic and political life, but only through a coalition of denominations, led by Anglicans, Presbyterians, and Methodists, and the armed might of the British army. The 500,000 Catholics who still choose to live and work in Ulster constitute the largest single religious group there. The Protestant coalition subsists on the vehement anti-Catholic sentiments of a people who dread giving the Catholics their social and political rights, fearing a Catholic takeover, a break with Britain, and reunification with southern Ireland.

In recent years, this seething cauldron of religious hatred has boiled over. The result

Top: Local residents get ready for the pope's arrival. Below: The pope is welcomed by dignitaries at the Dublin airport.

has been an orgy of violence that has left the guilty and the innocent lying side by side in the streets and gutters of Ulster. The tensions and dangers created by the problems in Ulster cannot be escaped anywhere in the Emerald Isle. For this reason, extreme security measures, the most extreme in the history of the whole island, were employed to assure protection of John Paul II. This tight protection was apparent not only on land but also in the sky. As the papal jet approached Dublin airport, it made a low pass over Phoenix Park, where over one million people from all over Ireland awaited the pontiff's arrival and the midday Mass he was to offer. Leading the *Saint Patrick,* flying in the formation of a cross, was a squadron of the Irish Air Force, French-made Mystère jet fighters under orders to shoot down any unidentified intruder into the papal airspace.

Earlier, in a brief departure ceremony at Rome's Leonardo da Vinci Airport, the pope had stated his reason for going to Ireland. "I hope," he said, "from the bottom of my heart that my visit helps to change the atmosphere of tension that especially in recent times has provoked lacerations and also, sad to say, ruin and death."

SEPTEMBER 29, 1979:
DUBLIN

As church bells tolled all over the fair city, and boats anchored in Dublin harbor blasted out their respects, John Paul stepped from the Aer Lingus jet. Removing his white zucchetto, he prostrated himself and kissed the Irish soil. Greeting him at the airport were Ireland's President Patrick Hillery, Prime Minister John Lynch, and the primate of all Ireland, Tomás Cardinal O'Fiaich (pronounced O-fee), whose see extends into Northern Ireland. The pope, though tired from the flight, was exuberant and cheerful.

From Dublin airport, the papal entourage, including eighteen special Vatican aides, flew by helicopter to the west side of Dublin and the sprawling, 1,700-acre Phoenix Park, across the Liffey River from the huge Guinness Brewery. Once a royal deer park, it is now a spaciously serene area of idyllic pleasure where one can run a gamut of pastoral joys, including following the steeplechase at the Phoenix Park Racecourse,

taking in the beautiful floral displays offered at the People's Flower Gardens, or looking at the host of animals on display at the Zoological Gardens, one of the best zoos in Europe. Moreover, within this wooded wonderland are the American embassy, the former Papal Nunciature, and the residence of the president of Ireland.

On the afternoon of September 29, however, this entire park, the largest enclosed park area in all of Europe, belonged to one man, Pope John Paul II. He used it to capacity, filling the natural amphitheater in which he spoke with his message of peace for this troubled isle. He showed a familiarity with Ireland's situation today by outlining the insubstantial nature of total allegiance to a technocracy that plays upon the naiveté of its victims through the habit-forming authority of the mass media. (Ireland had no television until 1961. Since its introduction to the island, both through Telefis Eireann, and the British television network, the BBC, it has had a profound effect on the social structure of the nation. Meanwhile, Ireland's entrance into the European Common Market in 1965 has lifted the economy and increased the well-being of the population. All this, however, has diverted attention away from religion and, according to the church's understanding of it, posed the danger of converting the nation to false, materialistic values.) "Prosperity and affluence," John Paul told the audience gathered to hear him in Phoenix Park, "even when they are only beginning to be available to a larger strata of society, tend to make people assume that they have a right to all that prosperity can bring, and thus they can become more selfish in their demands."

"Everybody," he continued, "wants full freedom in all the areas of human behavior, and new models of morality are being proposed in the name of would-be freedom. When the moral fiber of a nation is weakened, when the sense of personal responsibility is diminished, then the door is open for the justification of injustices, for violence in all its forms, and for the manipulation of the many by the few." He concluded this analysis by saying that the Irish people were being duped by this "temptation to accept as true freedom what in reality is only a new form of slavery." The rectifier and redeemer in all of this, as borne out by the evangelism of this vibrant pope, is the church, which historically has always been the hope and security of Ireland. To abandon the church now would simply mean destroying the secure bulwark the Irish people have depended on for deliverance since the fifth century.

Following the Mass at Phoenix Park, the pope then took to motorized transport for an evening tour of the Dublin center city; there countless Irish awaited him with reverent adoration. His parade took him along the quays of the Liffey River into the heart of Dublin, which had been transformed into a festive expression of love and respect: myriad papal flags were waved by cheering crowds along the modern and ancient streets of this 1,700-year-old city, whose walls were plastered with pictures of this dynamic man. More than two-thirds of the population of the republic plus hundreds of thousands from Northern Ireland were to see the Holy Father that day.

The motorcade moved across Parnell Square, by the Parnell Monument, dedicated to Charles Parnell, the one-time champion of Irish rights in the British Parliament during the 1880s. Then it went up O'Connell Street, and past the General Post Office where Patrick Pearse declared Ireland a republic, thus initiating what became known as the Easter Rising, and a civil war that was to last until the Anglo-Irish Treaty of 1922.

John Paul was ninety minutes behind schedule, a delay due to the overwhelming welcome of a people as warm, understanding, and adoring as any crowd he had encountered.

The magnificent cross at Phoenix Park
Below: The pope's motorcade is brought to a standstill by well-wishers.

DROGHEDA AND A PLEA FOR PEACE

The next stop on this pilgrimage was at Drogheda, some thirty miles north of Dublin and the closest point to the Northern Ireland border the pope would visit.

It was late evening by the time John Paul and his party arrived by helicopter on the fields of Killineer, just outside the town of Drogheda. There 400,000 admirers had waited patiently for him, and they greeted his arrival with warmth and respect, anticipating the seriousness of the homily of the Mass, which would ask the parties involved in the deadly strife in Northern Ireland to lay down their weapons and join in an all-out ecumenical effort for world peace.

Those who had gathered were a mixture of northern and southern Irish, and traffic along the major highways leading to Drogheda from Dublin and Belfast had been bumper to bumper for almost twenty-four hours.

In his dramatic homily, John Paul said firmly, "Peace cannot be established by violence; peace can never flourish in a climate of terror, intimidation and death." The crowd was hushed. The heavy darkness of the late, unusually warm evening seemed to intensify

stimulus to a solution of Ireland's problems.

In a way, this homily embodied the reason for the Irish pilgrimage. It touched upon the wound that has made this island weep with tears of blood. This Slavic pope, himself from a country with a history of violence and conquest, had, in this momentous forty minutes, conquered the conscience of a people, once described as "supreme individualists given to a natural bent toward rebellion."

After the Mass, John Paul, in a role that had earned him the title "the people's pope," waded into the throng to communicate directly with a people who through his presence, had become, in only a few hours, enthusiastic, joyous, and hopeful.

the reverence of the massive audience. They were aware that the pope was speaking sobering truths, given the unbridled violence and terror Ireland had suffered through most of her existence, especially in the last ten years.

Welcomed by both Catholic and Protestant religious leaders, he assured the Protestant people that he was a fellow Christian. Digging deep into the roots of the hatreds and hurts that separated the two communities in Northern Ireland, he said he had not come with a political message but with a strictly human and basically Christian consideration. Christ warned, "He who lives by the sword will perish by the sword!" Hence, he appealed to all those involved in the violence as the solution to their problems to put aside this totally unchristian behavior and to devote their efforts to an "authentic movement of peace and justice and of the mutual love that should exist between all of mankind everywhere."

Turning to the statesmen and politicians, he begged them to give their fullest attention to the problem of justice, dignity, and peace in this troubled land. He warned that if they failed to produce a solution they would see nothing but a continuation of the horrors now afflicting their country. Returning to his condemnation of violence, he said there was no way in which it could be accepted as a possible

SEPTEMBER 30, 1979: GALWAY AND THE KNOCK SHRINE

In the afternoon the pope and his entourage left Dublin, where John Paul had spent the night, for Galway and the Mass to be held there at the Galway Racecourse.

Galway is on the western coast of Ireland and is predominantly Gaelic in language and custom. It is a panoramic area, one where the wild, harsh, shore-pounding Atlantic Ocean clashes with the rolling emerald green of the countryside. Here the signs of welcome carried by the immense crowds and the banners that hung over the ocean-sprayed streets from the windows of churches and pubs alike proclaimed, "Jan Pawel II: Cead Mile Failte," a Gaelic phrase meaning "A Hundred Thousand Welcomes to John Paul II." And a hundred thousand welcomes he got, too, as once again a throng of Irish met him with their flashing smiles and warm greetings. The descendants of Celts, who came to this island in 350 B.C., they were the sons and daughters of King Brian Boru, Ireland's greatest ancient hero, who drove the Vikings from the shores of Erin in the Battle of Clontarf in 1014. Today, they were being treated to the presence of a genial man of good news, much grace, and bold, forthright diplomacy.

The Mass at the Galway Racecourse was

directed at the youth of Ireland, a group that constitutes almost 50 percent of the population. He again pleaded with them to avoid the enticements of bitterness, violence, and sectarian argument and to stick stoically to the way of the Gospel, the path of peace Christ opened up to the world through His gift of redemption.

After the Galway Mass and a motorcade that passed through the packed streets of the town of Galway, the pope went by helicopter into the hills of County Mayo to the unique and divinely mystical place called Knock. There, on August 21, 1879, more than a dozen villagers reported seeing a great globe of light that surrounded three holy figures identified as the Virgin Mary, Saint Joseph, and Saint John the Evangelist, as well as an altar on which lay a sacrificial lamb, all standing in the shadow of a large cross. After an inquiry commission failed to disprove, through any natural explanation, the meaning of this vision, the site began attracting pilgrims from all over Ireland; gradually, over the hundred years since, it became the most hallowed spot in the Emerald Isle. Now it is a national shrine and is housed in the largest church in Ireland, the Basilica of Our Lady, Queen of Ireland. The building is of a stadiumlike, circular design whose combined five chapels have a seating capacity of 15,000. Needless to say, there were many more than 15,000 on hand to embrace John Paul II in Irish camaraderie as he celebrated with them the 100th anniversary of the shrine, then went into one of the chapels to worship silently and alone for a few moments of communion with God and the Blessed Virgin.

From Knock, John Paul returned to Dublin by helicopter, there to meet with the Irish bishops and to take dinner with the nuns at the Cabra Dominican convent.

John Paul II passes on an overhead ramp shortly after his arrival at the shrine to the Virgin Mary at Knock.

OCTOBER 1, 1979:
MAYNOOTH AND LIMERICK

The short but singularly spectacular pilgrimage to Ireland was drawing to a close. Over three million people, nearly the entire population of Ireland, had come out to greet the pope and to accept him as one of their own. Jan Pawel had stirred their hearts and strengthened their Catholic faith. Moreover,

The American flag on display

A little girl plays contentedly with her souvenirs.

to the United States were hectic. It was a full, tight schedule, one that included first a visit to the great Saint Patrick's College at Maynooth, just northwest of Dublin. Here, beneath the college's Gothic spire, on the tree-shaded lawn, he made a brief address in which he called for the theologians and worshipers to unite within the Catholic church and go forth to spread the message of Christ's gift to mankind, a message of peace and goodwill on earth.

In his talks to the laity, nuns, priests, and bishops, John Paul had expressed his elation over the manifest faith that met him everywhere. He compared the fervor of the Irish faithful with that of his native Poles. At the same time, he could not ignore the prosperity that was obvious on all sides throughout the country, a result of the Republic of Ireland's joining the European Economic Community. Quite bluntly, the Holy Father had warned his fervent faithful that without vigilance and care they could easily slip into the secular attitude that seems an inevitable companion of material well-being.

From Maynooth, the papal party flew to Limerick, the fourth largest city in Ireland, an industrial and market town, a "bare spot," (the literal meaning of the word limerick) on the "vast, slow-moving" river Shannon, the major river of Ireland. Here, just below the great limestone plain that borders above this city, where Norman influence can still be seen in the ruins of King John's Castle near Thomond Bridge on the river Shannon, John Paul celebrated a Mass at the Greenpark Racecourse before a crowd estimated at about 200,000.

FAREWELL TO IRELAND

At Shannon International Airport, amidst still another great crowd of people, His Holiness bade farewell to the people of Ireland.

After again kissing the Irish soil, John Paul II boarded the Aer Lingus 747 *Saint Patrick*, bound for the final leg of this great adventure, his seven-day visit to the United States. The closing of the plane's door may have shut out the sounds of the cheering, exuberant Irish well-wishers at the airport, but it would never close off the memories he would carry in his heart of this trip.

he had forced them to stop and take notice of the consequences of the continuing strife with fellow Christians. He begged them to follow him in the pursuit of peace everywhere in the world, the mission he had set for himself upon his election in October, 1978. They responded with unanimous agreement: he was the catalyst that rekindled within them the desire for peace and brotherhood.

The remaining hours before his departure

6
AMERICA HAILS THE POPE

This was John Paul II's third trip to the United States. He had been there on two other occasions, once in 1969 and then again in 1976. Both times he went as Karol Cardinal Wojtyla. In September, 1969, he visited Polish-American churches, schools, convents, and hospitals on a whirlwind tour that carried him to New York, Connecticut, Ohio, Pennsylvania, Michigan, and Massachusetts.

The 1976 trip lasted three months: July, August, and September. At that time, he headed a delegation of Polish bishops attending the 41st International Eucharistic Congress in Philadelphia. The trip also included his lectures at Harvard, the University of Wisconsin, U.C.L.A., and the Catholic University of America, and took him to New Jersey, Maryland, Virginia, Michigan, New York, Massachusetts, Wisconsin, Illinois, California, Montana, and Canada.

One of the people he made friends with while on those two trips was his cousin, John Wojtyla, an auto worker, who later attended John Paul II's papal installation as a member of the United States delegation.

Officially, the trip represented another milestone in the pope's pilgrimage among the people of the world to deliver a message of peace and to call for the honoring of human dignity everywhere.

Boston, New York City, Philadelphia, Des Moines, Chicago, and, finally, Washington, D.C. were the cities to be honored by the pope's visit.

BOSTON

Geography alone suggests Boston as a good, logical place for Pope John Paul II's first stop on his pilgrimage to the United States. After all, no region of the country is closer to his point of departure, Ireland, than New England, and Boston is New England's largest city and its cultural and commercial center. That is why New Englanders have long called it "the Hub."

Boston has been called "the most Catholic city in the United States." Perhaps it is, but it wasn't always. The Puritans who fled England and founded the town in 1630

John Paul II arrives at Logan airport, Boston.

sought religious freedom, but they were not willing to extend it to others. The colony passed strict anti-Catholic laws, and not until 1780, during the American Revolution, did Catholics have the legal right to worship as they chose. Their number grew slowly but surely thereafter, and Pope Pius erected, in 1808, the diocese of New England, naming Jean Lefebvre de Cheverus as first bishop of Boston.

In the nineteenth century, the picture changed dramatically. Great masses of emigrants, many of them Catholics, went to America in search of a better life. They went from virtually every country of the Old World, but one group in particular had a remarkable impact on Boston life, the Irish. The greatest influx was in the late 1840s after a mysterious blight had struck the potato crop. Without the inexpensive, nutritious, easy-to-cultivate staple that had so helped the Irish survive poverty and exploitation, a million of them died between 1846 and 1849. Another million fled to North America, packed into boats that came to be known as "coffin ships" because so many passengers perished on the way over.

Irish immigrants flooded into Boston, especially into South Boston, a peninsula jutting into the Atlantic that was orginally intended as a residential area for the well-to-do. These immigrants, however, were not well-to-do. They were desperately poor and lacked skills and education. They had to rely on their own will, their capacity for hard work, and on the strength their Catholic faith gave them for the fight for a better life.

But they survived. The children of unskilled laborers and domestic servants became policemen, firemen, schoolteachers, letter carriers, contractors, lawyers, and doctors. One avenue of advancement was the church: it is said that South Boston has produced more priests and nuns than any comparable area of the country. Another avenue was politics, in which Irish-Americans began to display remarkable gifts. Beginning with the election of Hugh O'Brien in 1885 (ten years after the archdiocese of Boston had been created), the city had a fabled series of Irish mayors. One of the most remarkable was John F. "Honey Fitz" Fitzgerald, whose daughter Rose was to marry Joseph P. Kennedy, grandson of a poor Irish immigrant.

*In full regalia,
the band sends forth a
rousing welcome.*

*Senator Edward M. Kennedy
at Logan airport*

Kennedy went on to amass a great fortune and to dream of the day when one of his sons would become president of the United States. He had hoped it would be his eldest son, Joseph, Jr., who was killed tragically when his U.S. Navy plane exploded during a World War II mission. His second-born son, John F. Kennedy, thus became the one on whom the father's dream centered. Had he voiced it publicly, many would have scoffed at his hopes: no Catholic had ever been elected president, and if Al Smith's defeat in 1928 by Herbert Hoover was any indication, none ever would be. Happily, JFK's successful campaign in 1960 put that myth to rest once and for all, and it seemed fitting that the first Catholic president had his roots in Boston. To the nation's and the world's horror, President Kennedy was struck down by an assassin in 1963; five years later, his younger brother Robert met the same fate. Joseph Kennedy's only surviving son, Senator Edward M. Kennedy, was among the dignitaries at the airport to greet the Holy Father as he set foot on American soil.

*Exuberant onlookers wave from a
vantage point atop a highway sign.*

THE ARRIVAL AT LOGAN AIRPORT

Saint Patrick, the giant Aer Lingus 747 bearing Pope John Paul II to the United States, loomed out of the mist and touched down at Boston's Logan International Airport a few minutes before 3:00 P.M. on October 1. It was the first — and last — time the Holy Father would be on time in his U.S. visit. The archbishop of Boston, Humberto Cardinal Medeiros, climbed the ramp and disappeared into the plane to greet the pope. A few seconds passed, and then the pontiff appeared in the open doorway in his white cassock and red cape. He smiled benevolently and after carefully descending the stairs, knelt and kissed the ground in an ancient symbolic gesture before being greeted by the dignitaries awaiting him. Among them was the 102-year-old Monsignor Finn, who received a vigorous embrace from the Holy Father, and then reminded him that he had served the church under ten popes, from Pius IX to John Paul II.

The pontiff, Cardinal Medeiros at his side, was greeted by the first lady of the

United States, Rosalynn Carter, Massachusetts Governor Edward King and his wife, Speaker of the House Thomas P. O'Neill, Jr., and his wife, Massachusetts senators Edward M. Kennedy and Paul Tsongas and their wives, Boston Mayor Kevin White and his wife, and several other officials and political figures, including former House Speaker John McCormack. Then His Holiness was welcomed by the cardinals of North America and representatives of the National Conference of Catholic Bishops.

After he had made his way through the long receiving line of notables, the pope and Mrs. Carter exchanged official words of greeting.

Mrs. Carter's welcome was a gem of simple sincerity. "We welcome you to our country with love!" Wearing a neat black suit with a brimmed hat, giving her an almost Pilgrim air, she told the pope that he was no stranger since he had impressed himself on the whole world "as few have done before you."

"We welcome you with excitement," Mrs. Carter continued, in her soft, southern modulated tones, and praised the pope's visit as bringing a vision of all that unites mankind. Assuring him that he was deeply loved in America, she brought him the welcome and greetings of her husband, President Jimmy Carter.

John Paul II descending from the ramp of the Saint Patrick.

Wearing a poncho over his choir robe, the director leads the choir despite the rain.

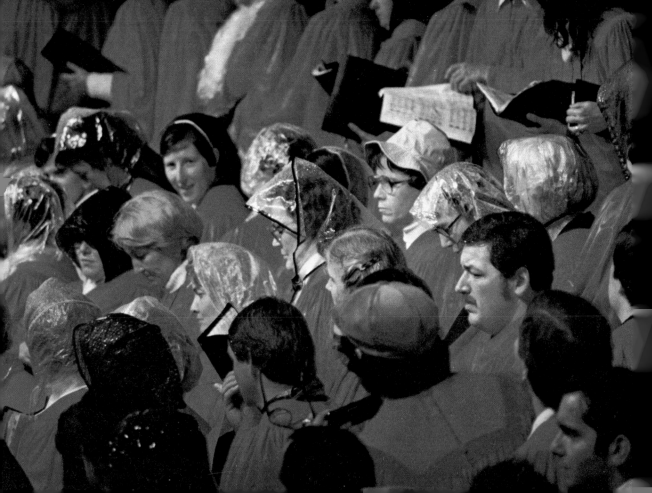

*The pope waves to the crowds
lining the street as the papal
motorcade makes its way
through the streets of Boston.*

*The official
medallion,
commissioned by
the Boston
archdiocese,
to commemorate the
historic visit of
Pope John Paul
to the city.*

*Below: Cheerful smiles are
evident as the guests move
along the receiving line,
umbrellas aloft.*

THE PAPAL MOTORCADE
THROUGH BOSTON

Now it was time for His Holiness to
enter the car that would take him on a
triumphant motorcade through the city.
The limousine left the airport and entered
nearby Sumner Tunnel, which connects
East Boston with the downtown area.
Minutes later, it emerged and swung down
Hanover Street, in the heart of Boston's
historic North End, to the unrestrained
delight of huge crowds. A light, misty rain
was falling, but no one cared; they were
there to rejoice, and rejoice they did!

The jubilation continued as the
motorcade swung down along the waterfront
and through famous old Boston Irish
neighborhoods: South Boston, Dorchester,
and the South End. Wearing a red, broad-
brimmed felt hat to protect himself from the
drizzle, the pope stood in the open car in
order to better exchange greetings and
glances of love with the enthusiastic
thousands on each side of his route.

The streets were decorated with gold and
white papal flags and homemade banners with
such messages as "Viva il Papa" ("Long Live
the Pope"), "Benvenuto al North di Boston,"
("Welcome to the North End of Boston"),
and "Cead Mile Failte" ("A Hundred Thousand
Welcomes"). Particularly ecstatic were the
parishioners of Our Lady of Czestochowa in
Dorchester, the oldest Polish church in the
city; after attending Mass, they lined up to
watch the first Polish pope ever pass within
feet of them.

At the Cathedral of the Holy Cross in the
South End, the motorcade stopped, and the
Holy Father entered the cathedral for a brief
but emotional service of prayer and greeting
with New England clergy. Two thousand
priests of the archdiocese responded as
he blessed them and praised them for
their dedication.

*Heads together, the pope
and Rosalynn Carter
exchange warm greetings.*

THE GREAT MASS
ON BOSTON COMMON

After the service, the motorcade began
to move toward Boston Common for the
great outdoor Mass that His Holiness would
celebrate there. The Common, the oldest
public park in the country, is located in the
center of the city on modestly sloping ground
that rises up to where the golden-domed
Massachusetts State House is situated.
As the pope approached, thousands were
beginning to gather for the papal Mass, the
first John Paul would celebrate in the United
States. Its theme was "Youth and the
Church," and space near the altar specially
constructed for the occasion had been
reserved for 10,000 young people of the area.

Space had also been reserved for
ecumenical representatives, including a
delegation of Protestant churchmen who
planned to present His Holiness with a cross

bearing the message (in Latin): "That we may
be one." The cross was symbolic of how
Protestant leaders throughout New England
welcomed the pope's visit; they called it an
"ecumenical celebration," and many urged
church members to contribute toward
helping the Catholic diocese defray the cost
it involved.

It was late in the afternoon and raining
when the pope arrived at the Common,
but nothing could dampen the joy of the
40,000 worshipers who had gathered there.
Preceded to the altar by a long procession of
servers, deacons, priests, bishops and
cardinals, the pope celebrated the Mass in
honor of Saint Therese of the Child Jesus,
one of the few saints canonized in this century,
whose feast is celebrated on October 1.

During his homily, he cried out, "I greet
you, America the Beautiful," and the huge
throng responded with cheers and cries of
"Viva il Papa." He paused and then, to the

*Yankee Stadium
New York City*

Saint Patrick's Cathedral

Waiting patiently for a glimpse of the pope, bystanders take shelter from the rain. Below: Papal flags were popular souvenir items.

delight of the crowd, spontaneously remarked, "Beautiful! Even if it rains!" He spoke of America's generosity and freedom and expressed his hopes for world peace, social justice, and human rights. Then he called upon the youth, whom he described as "the future of the world," to follow Christ. He warned against the escapism that many young people pursue in the face of problems and disappointments and then added, "I propose to you the option of love, which is the opposite of escape." He concluded with these inspiring words: "This is why I have come to Boston tonight: to call you to Christ — to call all of you and each of you to live in His body, today and forever. Amen!"

It was dark and raining heavily when the pope reached the communion of the Mass and then turned to offer it to others as hundreds of priests fanned out from the altar to reach those who wished to receive communion. Then, with a papal blessing and a ceremonial hymn, the Mass ended.

It had been a long day, one that began at 7:30 A.M. in Ireland (2:30 A.M. Boston time). Hence it was a tired Holy Father who entered the limousine that would take him to Cardinal Medeiros's residence for the night. The motorcade moved westward through the darkness, out broad, beautiful Commonwealth Avenue through the elegant Back Bay area and past Boston University. Then it reached Allston and finally Brighton, where the cardinal's residence is located. Despite his fatigue, the pope mingled with the crowd who had awaited his arrival with great patience in the rain. At long last His Holiness enjoyed a quiet dinner with a small group of clergy and retired for a well-earned rest.

FAREWELL TO BOSTON

He was up again, however, early the next morning. After a meeting with seminarians from Saint John's Seminary, he entered a helicopter that would take him to Logan airport for his 8:30 A.M. flight to New York City. At Logan, Trans World Airlines 727, named *Shepherd One* in recognition of the Holy Father's pastoral mission in the United States, carried him away from the love and the joy New England had expressed over his coming.

Nearly a million worshipers assembled for the pontifical Mass held on Boston Common.

OCTOBER 2, 1979:
NEW YORK CITY—THE UNITED NATIONS

*Pope John Paul II waves to the
crowd on the motorcade
enroute from the United Nations
to Saint Patrick's Cathedral.*

It dawned iron-gray the day John Paul II
arrived in New York. The best news about
the weather was that there was only a
30 percent chance of rain. The people of
New York City were, nevertheless, happy.
An estimated five million had gathered along
the parade routes: along the Grand Central
Parkway that would bring the pope into the
city proper from La Guardia Airport, when he
arrived from Boston at 9:10 A.M., and along
the East River Drive, down which his
entourage would travel, making its way to the
United Nations, where he was to address the
General Assembly at noon.

A crowd of 2,000 was on the tarmac
at La Guardia to meet him on his arrival.
Following a short welcome by UN Secretary-
General Kurt Waldheim, Pope John Paul II
stated that he had looked forward to this
visit ever since the secretary-general had
extended to him an invitation to speak before
the Thirty-fourth General Assembly at
the beginning of his pontificate. He also
reemphasized the purpose of his pilgrimage
to Ireland and the United States: to bring
together people of all races, colors, and creeds
into a one-world embodiment of peace.

When John Paul arrived at the United
Nations, he was met there by an exuberant
crowd of spectators, some waiting in the
concrete-walled and tiered plaza directly in
front of the UN complex on First Avenue.
He had been accompanied in his motorcade
from the airport by the secretary-general,
Terence Cardinal Cooke of New York,
archbishop Giovanni Cheli, the pope's
representative at the UN, and Bishop Francis
Mugavero of Brooklyn. The pope had made
the trip from the airport in an open-roof
limousine, in which he stood, extending his
greetings to the hundreds of thousands of
admirers lining the route.

After conferring with dignitaries in the
secretary-general's quarters, at noon,
John Paul went before the gathered assembly
to deliver his address.

At the United Nations, before a full
General Assembly (during Paul VI's address to
the assembly in 1965, the Albanian delegation
had not been in attendance — they were for

65

*A nun zeroes in on
the papal motorcade;
John Paul II
speaking at Saint
Patrick's Cathedral.*

this papal speech), John Paul II expounded his message of world peace by insisting that such peace could not be obtained through worker-enslaving economic systems or major-power armaments races.

Before he entered the assembly hall, he greeted the families of the various delegates and accepted a bouquet of flowers from a group of children from the International School, hugging, kissing, and blessing several of them as he did so.

At the beginning of his speech, he mentioned Paul VI and reinvoked his famous appeal to the countries of the world to put an end once and for all to war.

Again, as he had done in his greetings at La Guardia, he stressed his recommendation that the currently divided world must be directed toward a spirit of oneness. He stated that the United Nations exists to unify and associate, not divide and oppose. He was appearing before the General Assembly, a public address system that reaches all the people of the world. During the speech, he kept alluding to the "concrete individual" and the "universal"value of human life. "The Catholic church," he stated, "in every place on earth proclaims a message of peace, prays for peace, educates for peace."

The first world problem he covered was that of the Palestinian question and the territorial integrity of Lebanon, the settlement of which, he said, was imperative if there was to be peace in the Middle East. He specifically stated that he believed the city of Jerusalem, in determining this peace, should remain an international city, available to pilgrims of the three religions that hold it sacred: Judaism, Christianity, and Islam.

The main course of his speech centered around the question of the armaments race. "The continual preparations of war," he said, "demonstrated by the production of ever more numerous, powerful, and sophisticated weapons in various countries show that there is a desire to be ready for war, and being ready means being able to start it; it also means," he continued, "taking the risk that sometime, somewhere, somehow, someone can set in motion the terrible mechanism of general destruction.

"It is therefore necessary," he said, "to make a continuing and even more energetic effort to do away with the very possibility of provoking war and to make such catastrophes impossible by influencing

*New York senators
Daniel Patrick
Moynihan and Jacob
Javits in front of
Saint Patrick's
Cathedral*

enjoyed and drawn upon, the more, then, do those goods show their indestructible and immortal worth." He said that spiritual goods were revealed through works of creativity, "works of thought, poetry, music, and the figurative arts, fruits of man's spirit."

"Material goods," he said, "by their very nature provoke conditioning and division. The struggle to obtain these goods becomes inevitable in the history of humanity. If we cultivate this one-sided subordination of man to material goods alone, we shall be incapable of overcoming this state of need."

He has constantly said that work should inspire and not tire and considers economic tensions as those most contributory to the neuroses of both men and their societies. Economic competition breeds injustice, and injustice leads to war.

In concluding, he reiterated his belief that one of the most inalienable rights mankind has is its right to worship God as it so pleases. "All human beings," he said, "in every nation and country should be able to enjoy effectively their full rights under any political regime or system."

He ended this address to the General Assembly by pleading with the delegates to prevent passing on to the children of the world — especially important, he underlined, during the UN observance of the Year of the Child — the burden of the arms race and its possible catastrophic consequences.

After his address, John Paul, receiving a standing ovation from the delegates, sat at first with bowed head, revealing the tiredness that must have coursed through his body due to the exhausting demands of his rigorous schedule.

Following lunch at the Holy See Mission on East 72nd Street, the pope returned to the United Nations, where he met with members of the staff, delegates and dignitaries. Then John Paul II and the papal cadre journeyed the few blocks over to Saint Patrick's Cathedral on fashionable Fifth Avenue.

the attitudes and convictions, the very intentions and aspirations of governments and peoples." Observers saw this as a direct appeal to the countries involved in the SALT agreement, the United States and the Soviet Union, to accelerate the adoption of that treaty so that such a possible catastrophe as he described might be averted.

In the second most important part of his speech, John Paul expounded on the corrupting effects of materialism on mankind, a subject he first stressed during his historic trip to Poland in June, 1979. "It is easy to see," he said, "that material goods do not have unlimited capacity for satisfying the needs of man: they are not in themselves easily distributed and, in the relationship between those who possess and enjoy them and those who are without them, they give rise to tension, dissension, and division that will often even turn into open conflict."

He continued by saying, "Spiritual goods . . . are open to unlimited enjoyment by many at the same time, without diminution of the goods themselves, the more they are

AT SAINT PATRICK'S CATHEDRAL

The diehards of the pope's aficionados were waiting in front of Saint Patrick's Cathedral as early as 6:00 A.M. in order to catch at least a long moment's glance at this

Chicago

Washington, D.C.

New York's
Finest keep
the crowd back as
they wait for the
pope's arrival.

popular leader of the Catholic church. By
10:00 A.M., the various vendors, those selling
John Paul T-shirts, buttons, flags, and other
memorabilia, were hawking their wares with
loud vigor among the swelling crowds that
backed out into Fifth Avenue. All around the
cathedral, sidewalks and side streets had been
cordoned off by wooden barricades, and the
large contingent of police on duty, providing
His Holiness with the heaviest security yet,
were highly visible, as police had been
throughout the series of visits that began in
Dublin on September 29. Bostonians had
braved pea-soup mists and downpours to
welcome the pope, and in New York, too,
the people seemed willing to suffer any
discomfort to be present at the various papal
appearances scheduled to take place during
the two-day visit.

Behind the cathedral, high up on the
girders of a new hotel under construction,
workers cheered, whistled, and waved at
His Holiness from above a large, handsome
gonfalon that read, "Hardhats welcome the
Pope." The pope, seemingly surprised by their
enthusiasm, raised his arms toward them,
and smiled happily. In front of the cathedral,
where the crowds were thickest, again it was
the children who gained the pope's warmest
attention as they offered him gifts of flowers

in return for his embrace and blessing.

Inside the cathedral, before an audience
of invited guests, the pope offered prayers
after being welcomed by Terence Cardinal
Cooke. Followed by Cardinal Cooke, he then
made his way back out and around the
one-hundred-year-old church to continue
acknowledging the warm appreciation of the
people. Across Fifth Avenue, high up in the
windows of the buildings of Rockefeller
Center, admirers waved to him, took pictures
of him, and cheered his presence. He then
retired to Cardinal Cooke's residence for a
bit of rest before his evening schedule began.

IN HARLEM AND THE SOUTH BRONX

Two areas of the greatest social concern

*The students of Saint Aloysius
in Harlem reach out to
John Paul II.*

were visited by the pope in New York City.
The first was in Harlem and the second in the
South Bronx, both areas of extreme human
deprivation and frustration due to the
depressed and, in some cases, outright blighted
conditions of the environment.

A little after six, the papal party visited
the Saint Charles Borromeo Church, a Gothic
piece of elegant architecture sitting like a sore
thumb in a neighborhood more rubble than
upright, at 11 West 141st Street in the troubled
heart of Harlem. Built originally for a
predominantly Irish Catholic congregation in
the late 1880s, it is now home to 1,500 black
Catholics and is pastored by Monsignor
Emerson Moore. Monsignor Moore calls black
Catholics "a minority within a minority," but
felt that the pope's visit to his church was
just what was needed to reinstill Catholic
fervor within the community, a community
that has within its perimeters approximately
50,000 black Catholics.

At the church, Pope John Paul mingled
with the people spilling out of the packed
interior on to the steps and sidewalk,
stopping to accept flowers and a Polish
greeting from two young black girls who had
come to see him. Inside the church, he received
a rousing welcome as the congregation

encouraged him in his pastoral message with
reverberating praise and cheer.

From Harlem, the procession moved on
to the South Bronx, to an area that is sadly
one of the most poverty-stricken city zones
in the United States, one that must have
reminded the pope of the war-ravaged look
of his native Poland during World War II.
Here he came to bless the ground of a lot on
which the Catholic church is sponsoring the
construction of a housing project. The area is
a mixture of ethnic groups, predominantly
Puerto Rican. Respecting this, John Paul
gave a short speech in Spanish after being
introduced by Father James E. Connery,
the vicar of the South Bronx.

John Paul II and
President Jimmy Carter

They waited. The anticipation had the 80,000 people filling the house that Ruth built ready to applaud and cheer the slightest movement around the entrance to Yankee Stadium turned cathedral for this one night. When a contingency of police moved in to take their positions in readiness for the pontiff's appearance, they received a brief but tumultuous response from people in the nearby stands.

Finally, at ten minutes of nine, John Paul II appeared in a specially modified Ford Bronco pickup for a ride around the stadium.

One hundred carpenters had worked all night to construct the platform on which the pope was to say Mass. The stadium was dominated by a vast expanse of red carpet rolling up the aisle to spread over the whole platform. Around the platform blossomed several hundred yellow and white flowers planted within 300 potted shrubs. It was a photographer's holiday, and all around the stadium during the ceremonies, flashbulbs winked, popped, and twinkled, capturing the moment.

The celebration of the Eucharist went smoothly. A beautifully passionate "Gloria" was sung by two singers playing guitars, backed by the large choir and orchestra assembled especially for this Mass. During the Liturgy of the Word, the first reading was given by veteran actress Helen Hayes, who admitted before time that she was so nervous she had decided to read her passage rather than recite it.

In his homily, the pontiff dwelt on the subject of charity, telling the affluent to share with their poor brothers and sisters. "You must treat them," John Paul said, "like guests at your family table." He underlined his theme by using the "Parable of the Rich Man and Lazarus," saying that the rich man was condemned not because he was rich, but because he did not take care of the beggar. "God curses selfishness," the pope said in conclusion, tying the message in with one of his basic contentions, that the contemporary world is split by a striving for material goods, and that today's class struggle is between those who have and those who have not. He put forth that the world cannot afford to stand idly basking in whatever wealth it has accumulated while thousands of its unfortunate are starving to death.

Under a golden canopy, John Paul II delivers his homily at Yankee Stadium.

The scoreboard lights form the papal seal.

John Paul's first day in New York City was over. It had been a long day, one of definitely taxing duration for His Holiness, but one which the people of this great city had thoroughly enjoyed. He had won their hearts, and though the skies were overcast, the sunshine John Paul brought through his personal charm was enough to give the day a spring-like quality.

OCTOBER 3, 1979:
THE SECOND DAY IN NEW YORK CITY

John Paul's day started with a prayer service at Saint Patrick's Cathedral in the presence of 10,000 nuns, priests, and onlookers filling the church and the streets around the church. He was in a particularly jovial mood, and after he had led a group of nuns in song from the steps of the cathedral, he leaned into the microphone, smiled, and said, in that deep baritone voice of his, "Very nice."

On the way to his limousine for the trip to Madison Square Garden, he called a young boy from the crowd to hug him a moment, showing, as he does so often in his appearances, his great affection for children, of whom he has said in one of his poems, "The pulse of mankind beats in their hearts."

AT MADISON SQUARE GARDEN

The scene suddenly changed. But as drastically as it changed, so, too, it developed into one of the most touching of his New York visit, and what could become one of the most memorable moments of the trip for him.

At Madison Square Garden in the heart of Manhattan, he was greeted by 19,000 high school students who gave him a most unusual

Long streamers of ticker tape and computer cards tossed from windows above rain down on the papal motorcade and bystanders alike.

welcome. It was a time of young fun, a time set to the music of American youth, including a band performing such tunes as the theme from the movie *Superman,* and a collection of disco and rock melodies. As John Paul appeared on the podium the teenagers sang "Follow Me," "I Am the Bread of Life," "Alabare," and the theme from "Star Wars." A laser light show set the Garden ablaze with sparkling color, and the pope voiced his amazement of the whole, spontaneous reception with the Polish "Woooooohh!" the equivalent of shouting "Wow!" in English.

And a "wowing" moment it was for him and the teenagers. He was the guest of these young people and they meant for him to sit back and enjoy their show. They offered him a slide show that told him what life was like in their everyday world. Then followed a musical program, and a presentation of gifts. Among the gifts these teenagers gave John Paul were a guitar, a tape recording of special music performed by young people from the metropolitan area, a pair of blue jeans, a T-shirt with the words "The Big Apple

The passing scene: the clergy arrives for the occasion.

The papal motorcade in New York

A newscaster broadcasts from the scene.

Welcomes Pope John Paul II," and two handmade medallions: one a decoupage on wood showing an American flag, pictures of students, and a photo of Earth as seen from space; and the other an icon made of brass. Great jubilation rose from the young people when John Paul placed one of the medals around his neck. His message to these teenagers was one espousing the importance of a Catholic education.

A TICKER TAPE PARADE DOWN BROADWAY AND BATTERY PARK

John Paul emerged from Madison Square Garden into a downpour. Riding in his open-roof limousine, standing under an umbrella held by Terence Cardinal Cooke, who had been by his side throughout this visit, John Paul faced the rain stoically as his procession paraded down Broadway before a throng of thousands lining the street, three rows deep in some places. From above, from out of the thousands of open windows surrounding the scene, workers rained down pounds and pounds of computer cards and long streamers of ticker tape. From the street people tossed red and white carnations onto the roof and hood of the papal limousine (red and white are the national colors of Poland).

AT BATTERY PARK

In lower Manhattan's Battery Park the crowd stood in defiance of the rain to listen to John Paul greet them. While the Statue of Liberty seemed ghost-like through the mists of New York harbor behind them, the pontiff reemphasized his determined concern for the poor of the world, directing Americans to turn away from consumerism in favor of a direction leading to charity and brotherhood. "I appeal to all who love freedom and justice to give a chance to all in need," he said, "to the poor and the powerless. No institution or organization can credibly stand for freedom today if it does not also support the quest for justice." He concluded by saying, "Every nation has its historical symbols. Their significance lies in the truths they represent to the citizens of a nation and in

the image they convey to other nations. Such a symbol in the United States is the Statue of Liberty. This is an impressive symbol of what the United States has stood for from the very beginning of its history; this is a symbol of freedom."

He then called for an end to anti-Semitism and offered a special greeting to the New York Jewish community. After giving God's blessing to New York, he returned to his limousine to enter the homestretch of what had been a most unusual, heartwarming, and overwhelmingly successful visit for him.

BROOKLYN, SAINT JAMES' CATHEDRAL, SHEA STADIUM, AND OFF TO PHILADELPHIA

On the way to Shea Stadium and his final meeting with New Yorkers before his United States pilgrimage continued on to Philadelphia, Pope John Paul stopped in front of Saint James' Cathedral in the Borough Hall section of Brooklyn, the nation's fourth largest city. There he greeted a group of Polish youngsters from the Saint Stanislaus Kostka Church school in the Greenpoint section of Brooklyn. They met him dressed in native Polish costumes and shouted "Sto Lat!" or "May You Live a Hundred Years," a cheer he had heard continuously during his earlier trip to Poland.

At Shea Stadium, he said his farewell, again going over the basic reason for his coming to the United States: to instill within both Catholics and non-Catholics alike a passion for human dignity. At one point he injected another dose of his famous humor. In calling out the various boroughs represented in the audiences, he paused before the last one, then looked up and smiled. "And...Brooklyn," he said, raising his arms high in the air as he did so. The crowd responded with raucous delight.

His visit to New York City was ended. It had been an active, exhausting visit that had made him an honorary New Yorker in the sight of the millions who turned out to offer him their love and respect.

Banners and signs of welcome were assembled to greet the pope in Philadelphia.

PHILADELPHIA

Though less than 100 miles from New York City, the metropolis of Philadelphia is a completely separate entity, a great city in its own right, with its own distinctive history, economic and cultural life, and character. Visitors to the city are usually impressed, sometimes even surprised, by its gracious charm. One of those so charmed was Karol Cardinal Wojtyla on two visits to the city while archbishop of Krakow.

His first visit, in 1969, was highlighted by a stop at the Shrine of Our Lady of Czestochowa in nearby Doylestown, Pennsylvania. His second visit was occasioned by the Forty-First International Eucharistic Congress in 1976. This great conference, attended by more than a million people, was largely devoted to mankind's great "hungers," that is for God, bread, justice, the Holy Spirit, truth, understanding, peace, and Christ, the very same hungers to which Pope John Paul II has addressed himself so diligently and eloquently.

The visitor from Poland was undoubtedly well aware of Philadelphia's special place in American and Catholic American history. It was there, after all, that the United States was born through a declaration that said (in part): "We hold these truths to be self-evident, that all Men are created equal, that they are endowed by their Creator with certain inalienable rights, that among these are Life, Liberty, and the Pursuit of Happiness..."

In 1979, Pope John Paul was attracted back to Philadelphia not only by his affection for the city but also by his close friendship with the archbishop, John Joseph Cardinal Krol. The two have much in common. Both have parents who were from the Tatra Mountain region of southern Poland (though Cardinal Krol was born in Cleveland, Ohio); both were made cardinals on the same day in 1967; and both share the same views, which could be described as a mixture of liberalism and conservatism of the church and its role in the modern world. The pope was to enunciate some of these views — especially what some regard as the more conservative ones — more explicitly in Philadelphia than in either Boston or New York. Cardinal Krol is said to have played a major role in the decision by the 1978 conclave to elect Karol Wojtyla as the first Polish pope.

THE ARRIVAL AND MOTORCADE
TO THE CATHEDRAL

The pope was late on his arrival in Philadelphia. *Shepherd One* landed a little past 3:00 P.M. on October 3. But no one minded, since the delay gave the clouds a chance to clear and reveal a glorious blue sky.

The Supreme Pontiff descended the ramp from his plane, arm in arm with his close friend, Cardinal Krol. The first thing he saw was a sight that delighted him: 3,000 young people from the area's parochial grade and high schools. Seven hundred of them held up placards that formed a gigantic American flag bearing the message "Philadelphia Welcomes Pope John Paul II With Love." On signal, they reversed the placards to form another huge flag bearing the same message, this time in Polish! At one point, he plunged into the throng of delighted youngsters, waving a bouquet of yellow chrysanthemums.

After being greeted by Pennsylvania Governor Richard Thornburgh, Philadelphia Mayor Frank Rizzo and his wife, and the four auxiliary bishops of Philadelphia, the Holy Father entered an open-top limousine for a motorcade northward up Broad Street to the Cathedral of Saints Peter and Paul. Exuberant, cheering crowds lined the way not only in fiercely, loyally Catholic "South Philly," home to some 250,000 Italian-Americans, but also in "Center City." Wherever the Holy Father glanced, he saw his path bright with flags, banners, and smiling, laughing, joyful people— at least a million of them.

At last, he reached the cathedral, where he conducted a short prayer service for 2,000 holders of treasured gold tickets. During the service, he said "I thank the Lord for permitting me to come back to this city of Philadelphia....I feel very much at home in your midst....I am truly among friends."

THE MASS IN LOGAN CIRCLE

As the pope was preparing for the great outdoor Mass to be held in front of the cathedral, a crowd estimated at close to one million, gathered along broad, beautiful Benjamin Franklin Parkway. He celebrated the Mass on a red-and-gold carpeted platform nearly three stories high, built atop the

The vast expanse of red carpet leads to the platform at Logan Circle.

Priests hold the bread and wine to be distributed during Mass at Logan Circle.

One million faithful participate in the Mass at Logan Circle.

Logan Circle fountain and banked with thousands of chrysanthemums. Around him were forty bishops, clad in vestments of antique gold moiré taffeta with red velvet yokes and gold trim. During the ceremony, he descended the platform stairs to administer communion to some 150 children and adults while several hundred priests gave communion to other worshipers in the crowd.

In his homily the pope spoke of freedom and human values. He stressed, however, that freedom cannot be seen as "a pretext for moral anarchy" and decried present-day tendencies toward "laxity regarding the Christian view on sexuality." He said, "Moral values do not militate against the freedom of the person...on the contrary, they exist precisely for that freedom, since they are given to insure the right use of freedom."

When the two-hour Mass ended close to 7:00 P.M., the pope reentered his limousine for a drive along the city's beautiful West River Drive to Cardinal Krol's residence for dinner. Featuring Atlantic salmon and preceded by an old Philadelphia favorite, pepperpot soup, it was a rich, full meal after a rich, full day. The day, however, was not over. After dinner, he went to nearby Saint Charles Borromeo Seminary where he told the seminarians, "You must keep your promise to Christ, no matter what difficulties you may encounter." The visit was a happy and lighthearted encounter as the seminarians cheered and applauded and laughed with this warm, gentle friend.

OCTOBER 4, 1979: SAINT JOHN NEUMANN

Pope John Paul was scheduled to leave Philadelphia during the morning of October 4, but there was so much to do before his departure. First, there was a stop at the Redemptorist Fathers' Shrine of Saint John Neumann at Saint Peter's Church. John Neumann was the bishop who led the diocese of Philadelphia from 1852 until his death in 1860. Born in Bohemia (now Czechoslovakia) in 1811, he was ordained soon after going to America in 1836. Though he felt unqualified to be bishop of Philadelphia, he accepted the appointment and pursued his responsibilities vigorously and successfully. Parochial school

Mass for nearly 17,000 priests, seminarians, and religious at Philadelphia's Civic Center, where his homily addressed the issues of celibacy and the role of women.

Saint Charles Borromeo Seminary

John Paul II speaking at the Cathedral of the Immaculate Conception

enrollment, for instance, rose from 500 to 9,000 in the first two years of his episcopate. Philadelphians long ago began gathering the evidence that led to canonization — proof of the worthiness of his life and of three miracles resulting from his intercession.

Pope John Paul prayed in the basement sanctuary in which the remains of Saint John Neumann are encased behind glass. Then he went to the main upper church, where he gave a blessing, this time in Spanish.

From there, it was a short three blocks to the Cathedral of the Immaculate Conception, the cathedral of the Ukrainian Rite archdiocese of Philadelphia. Two thousand people crowded into the beautiful golden-domed structure to see and hear the pope. It is said that Ukrainian Rite Catholics often feel ignored by the Latin Rite or Roman Catholics who so outnumber them. The Holy Father's visit was a sign that they were not being overlooked, that he was *their* pope, too.

Pope John Paul's last stop in Philadelphia was the Civic Center, where he celebrated Mass for nearly 17,000 priests, seminarians, and members of religious orders. In his homily, the pope said that biblical tradition dictated that priests must remain celibate and that it is not women's role to be called to the priesthood, adding that this is "not a statement about human rights, nor an exclusion of women from holiness and mission in the church."

When the Mass ended, it was time to depart for the airport. There were new sights to see, new millions to greet. However, Philadelphians knew that their city held a special place in Pope John Paul's heart — and were proud.

Against a background of silos, Pope John Paul II walks on the grounds of the Living History Farms Museum near Des Moines, Iowa.

Saint Patrick's Church, Cumming, Iowa

OCTOBER 4, 1979: DES MOINES, IOWA

"The corn is as high as an elephant's eye" this time of year in Iowa, and the pigs are fat and ready to be trucked to market. Farm activity is at its peak. It is harvest time, and most Iowans have to plan their schedules accordingly. But for four hours on Thursday, October 4, those schedules were set aside. Iowans had something more important to attend to, and it was all because a Catholic farmer in Truro, Iowa, sat down one day last July and wrote a letter.

Joe Hays, a thirty-eight-year-old farmer who supports his family and farm by working full time at the John Deere tractor plant in Des Moines, gave his letter to Bishop Maurice L. Dingman while attending a church picnic near the end of July. Bishop Dingman accepted the letter but at first was puzzled as to just what to do with it. The letter was a handwritten invitation to Pope John Paul II. Joe Hays thought that since the Holy Father was going to the United States to get acquainted with its people and since he was going as close as Chicago, anyway, he shouldn't miss a chance to visit Des Moines and view America's heartland. Bishop Dingman put the letter aside for a few days, but Joe was insistent. He said he had been led by the Holy Spirit to write the letter. He was so sincere, that Bishop Dingman decided he could no longer put off trying to fulfill the farmer's request of him. Besides, by now, Bishop Dingman thought the idea a splendid one. So he sent the letter through the proper channels to the pope at the Vatican.

As it turned out, the letter was able to change the ambience of the entire state of Iowa for a brief four hours on Thursday,

October 4. For instead of ignoring the invitation to visit America's rural lands, John Paul was "thrilled" by the idea and proceeded to send Vatican advance man Bishop Paul Marcinkus to check out the facilities and arrangements in the Des Moines area. He was impressed by what he found, and the trip was on.

It happened that bright afternoon of October 4. There was only a slight nip in the air, and unlike the visits to Boston and New York City, the weather was given little consideration. After the big TWA jet, *Shepherd One*, landed at Des Moines Airport, the papal party was ferried by helicopter to the west side of the city to a 600-acre museum consisting of three different model farms called Living History Farms. He was greeted there by 350,000 people — 100,000 more than the entire population of Des Moines, the capital of Iowa — gathered in a natural amphitheater on the grounds of the farms, the largest crowd ever to witness any kind of event in Iowa history.

The first person to meet the pope at the Living History Farms was Joe Hays, the man whose letter had precipitated the Holy Father's visit.

It was the feast day of Saint Francis of Assisi, and in his homily during the Mass he celebrated before this large assembly, John Paul said it was the moral obligation of all farmers to feed the hungry first; in doing so, they would be blessed by more bountiful harvests. He said that American farmers were especially endowed and as such owed the world a share of their abundance.

Several people from all walks of American life, including an American Indian and a southern black, participated in communion.

Then, in a most unusual move, perhaps the most unique of the trip, the pope journeyed by National Guard helicopter to Cumming, Iowa, where he held a short service in the 111-year-old Saint Patrick's Church, a barnlike, wooden structure sitting gracefully in the cornfields on the rolling plains around it. After landing in a hay field owned by John and Marilyn Connor, John Paul amused the 204 farm-belt parishioners, most of them of Irish descent, by joking with their new, part-time pastor, the Reverend John Richter. In his speech, John Paul called the church and its congregation "a place and symbol of prayer and fellowship, the heart of a real Christian

community where people know each other personally, share each other's problems, and give witness together to the love of Jesus Christ. How "privileged," he continued, "you are that, in such a setting, you can worship God together. May the simplicity of your life-style and the closeness of your community be the fertile ground for a growing commitment to Jesus Christ."

After the pope had left for Chicago from Des Moines, Iowans expressed their sentiments concerning this great evangelist and humanitarian. They felt good about having been so important a part of history, the most exciting moment in Iowan memory, an event more far-reaching and long lasting than the 1959 visit to Des Moines by Soviet premier Nikita Khrushchev. "The pope beats Khrushchev all to pieces," said one Des Moines resident who was an on-the-spot witness to both visits. John Paul's presence lingered in the twilight, hovering over the fields and hills on that fall day. At Saint Patrick's Church, one parishioner put it best by saying the pope had left them with a feeling of "ecstasy." For four short hours, he had planted the seeds of peace among them. In ecstasy, those seeds are now growing.

A quiet interlude of worship at services held by the pope at Saint Patrick's Church, Cumming, Iowa. Below: Touring the grounds at the Living History Farms Museum

A golden rope holds
back the crowd.

The pope takes off
his hat to the crowd.

Clergy of many
denominations
listen to the
pope's message.

CHICAGO

The chill of autumn reached Chicago before the pope did, and many of the dignitaries waiting for his arrival at O'Hare International Airport began to shiver as they were buffeted by unseasonably cold winds. They had to wait longer than some of them had anticipated, too: the plane was originally scheduled to arrive at 6:00 P.M., but *Shepherd One* did not actually get in until about an hour and a half later. In other words, the pope was — as so often on this trip — late, but with all he had to experience and accomplish in Boston, New York, Philadelphia, and Des Moines, it was a tribute to his energy and stamina that he was as close to schedule as he was.

Among those at the airport to greet him were John Cardinal Cody, Illinois Governor James R. Thompson, Jr., Chicago Mayor Jane M. Byrne, and other Chicago luminaries. Warmed by his presence, they immediately forgot the chill weather. However, realizing what he had to accomplish that evening, His Holiness did not address those at the airport. Perhaps he felt it more important to enter his car and move toward the city, toward the hundreds of thousands of people who had been lining up along his route — some of them for hours — in the cold of nightfall.

His limousine sped down the expressway and then passed through the Polish-American neighborhood along Milwaukee Avenue. His reception was, if anything, even more ecstatic than had been expected. He was wildly cheered, thousands of bouquets were tossed, and his security forces repeatedly had to move swarms of people gently back so that the motorcade could proceed. How many were there in the throngs that stood ten and twenty deep beside his route? There are some 500,000 Polish-Americans in Chicago, and it seems as if they *all* were there, plus thousands of others of every race, creed, and ethnic background.

The pope's first destination was Holy Name Cathedral in downtown Chicago for a ceremony of welcome and prayer. The thousands who had been waiting inside for him greeted his arrival with cheers and songs. He moved toward the altar and paused for a few moments of silent prayer. Then he sat and heard the voice of Luciano Pavarotti

Pope John Paul II arriving in Chicago

A beautiful madonna and child on display for the papal motorcade

open the services with Schubert's "Ave Maria."

Later, the Holy Father spoke briefly, expressing his happiness at being back in Chicago once again. (The city was one of several he visited during trips to America in 1969 and 1976.) He observed that Chicago is not only "an American city" but also the "second Polish city in the world." (The first, of course, is Warsaw.) At this, the audience erupted into wild, deafening applause. He also said to them, with obvious and moving sincerity, "How greatly I would like to meet you in your homes, to walk your streets, so that I may better understand the richness of your personalities and the depth of your aspirations."

His listeners, quite naturally, tried to persuade him to stay longer with their cheers and applause. At long last, however, he took the microphone and good-naturedly announced that he had another appointment to keep that evening. Then he left for Saint Peter's Church, several blocks south of the cathedral, where he addressed a gathering of religious brothers. After the meeting, his limousine drove north, heading for the Gothic mansion that is Cardinal Cody's residence, where John Paul would find rest after a day that had begun many hours, and two cities, earlier.

OCTOBER 6, 1979:
THE PROVIDENCE OF GOD CHURCH

October 6 was yet another day of triumph for Pope John Paul. Everywhere he went, he passed great crowds of enthusiastic, exuberant people. Indeed, as his car emerged from the cardinal's residence, he saw a throng of well-wishers who had waited through the chilly predawn hours to see and greet him as he left at about 7:00 A.M. for the morning's missions. His route led, by design, through some of Chicago's poorer neighborhoods to the Providence of God Church, which is located in the so-called Pilsen community, once home to many Lithuanian immigrants who built the church. Today, the area is a poor, predominantly Mexican neighborhood.

Over the last ten years, however, it and many other poor neighborhoods have received spiritual and monetary support from the American Council of Bishops' Campaign for Human Development. The pope's visit to the church was in honor of the tenth anniversary of the campaign, whose national representatives were on hand inside the church to greet him. Outside stood the people of the neighborhood, who had worked hard to make sure that the church and the area around it were spotlessly clean. Of necessity, the Holy Father could spend only a few minutes at Providence of God, but his encounter with the people of Pilsen was an emotional, heartwarming experience. There were many who wept, while others cheered as His Holiness said first, "Good-by," and then, "Hasta la vista," before moving on.

THE POLISH MASS AT THE CHURCH OF THE FIVE HOLY MARTYRS

The pope's next stop was one that had been anticipated eagerly both by those who were present and by the Holy Father himself, for his limousine took him to the Church of the Five Holy Martyrs in southwest Chicago. In a sense, the church is the heart of Brighton Park, an inner-city neighborhood that is inhabited almost completely by Polish-Americans. Today, Poland's own Karol Wojtyla, the Supreme Pontiff of the Catholic church — was coming to the Church of the Five Holy Martyrs to conduct a prayer service and then to celebrate an outdoor Mass in Polish in the parking lot behind the church. For days, the community had been preparing for the visit; one of the last tasks to be accomplished was perhaps the most important: putting a huge cross into place beside the fifty-foot altar erected for the Mass. Thousands packed themselves together as close as they could to the altar. There were not only people from the neighborhood but also their friends and relatives from other Chicago neighborhoods and the suburbs and from the large Polish-American communities in outlying areas like Detroit, Milwaukee, and St. Louis.

The Mass was everything hoped for — and more. It was a celebration of their history, their culture, their pride, and their religion. The singing, happy crowd radiated a joy that had, if anything, been intensified by waiting through the cold, early-morning

The outdoor Mass at the Church of the Five Holy Martyrs

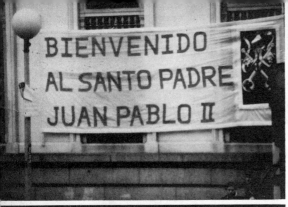

BIENVENIDO AL SANTO PADRE JUAN PABLO II

POLSKA
WARSZAWA
LWÓW
TARNOPOL
KOŁOMYJA
WILNO

Chicago loves the sweet Christ on earth Pope John Paul UNIV

ECH BĘDZIE POCHWALONY JEZUS CHRISTUS

POPE JOHN PAUL II
Worldwide Marriage Encounter
Your hope for the future is here.

JUS A WOMAN'S PLACE IS IN THE SANCTUARY

JUS HAS GENDER

We Are One

WELCOME Pope John Paul II from Holy Angels Academy BUFFALO

POPE JOHN PAUL II STO LAT NIECH ŻYJE

WE L
YO

HARLEM WELCOMES POPE JOHN PAUL II

WELCOME POPE JOHN PAUL

LIQUOR
WITAMY OJCA SWIĘTEG

STO LAT
NIECH ŻYJE NAM

ILLINOIS AIR NATIONAL GUAR
..ome's POPE JOHN PAUL II
WITAMY ŚWIĘTEGO OJCA
..ZCZE POLSKA NIE ZGINEL

HARDHATS WELCOME THE POPE

GAYS FOR THE POPE

DIGNITY
GAY/LESBIAN CATHOLICS
WELCOMES THE POPE

HARD HATS WELCOME JOHN PAUL II TO PHILA

BISHOP KEARNEY HIGH SCHOOL

VIVA IL PAPA

CARPENTERS WELCOME THE POPE NEW YORK
A HELMSLEY HOTEL OPENING...

SEXISM IS A SIN

JESUS WANTS YOU

WOMENS PLACE IS IN THE SANCTUARY

POPE JOHN PAUL: WITH YOU, WE WILL, BY THE GRACE OF GOD, RESTORE MORALITY!

THOU SHA NOT KILL JESUS WAS VEGETARIAN

Visit ... Old Chicago Smoke Shop
... Clark Street
WELCOME POPE
JOHN PAUL II

MAGDALEN COLLEGE loves POPE JOHN PAUL II

Chicago's office buildings form a backdrop for
the tradition and ceremony of the papal Mass.

hours for the pope to appear. John Paul
delighted them when he mentioned the general
belief that "he who rises early in the morning
will be sleepy all day," and then added,
"Maybe there's a little truth in this, but we're
going to hold on to the old Polish adage,
'He who rises early in the morning will receive
generously from God!'"

THE POPE'S REMARKS TO
THE BISHOPS OF THE UNITED STATES

After the Polish Mass, his motorcade
moved along Richmond Avenue, past more
adoring crowds, to Quigley South Seminary
to attend a special session of the United States
Bishops' Conference. Virtually the entire
hierarchy of the American church was present,
and his remarks to them made headlines,
for they touched upon several matters of great
moment to both Catholics and non-Catholics
today. He indicated his adherence to
traditional Catholic opposition to
contraception. He affirmed the belief that
marriage is an "indissoluble" and "irrevocable"
covenant. He expressed his opposition to
abortion and euthanasia. He referred to a
distinction that has been drawn between
homosexual "orientation" and homosexual
"acts," and agreed that the "orientation"
might not be immoral but that the "acts"
surely are. In making these points, the pope
quoted from a pastoral letter written by the
bishops three years earlier, a letter that
expressed the very views he endorsed.
Nevertheless, the reaction to his remarks was
hardly unanimous: some of those present
felt that his views on these matters are too
conservative and perhaps too far from what
many American Catholics feel and believe
today; others were pleased by the pope's clear,
firm commitment to moral positions long
associated with Roman Catholicism.

While the majority of the bishops
received these remarks with gratitude, a small
minority felt that many of these statements
did not confront the real problems in these
matters faced by the majority of American
Catholics. In the press the reaction was mostly
negative. Some commentators spoke of the
"end of the honeymoon period." But these
statements in no way diminished the
enthusiastic reception John Paul received

*iests in procession
Grant Park*

everywhere he went. People seemed to make a distinction between the papal message and the man of Christ who was visiting them.

●

THE MASS IN GRANT PARK

It was early afternoon when the session with the bishops ended, and the pope had planned a brief rest at the cardinal's residence before the great outdoor Mass he would celebrate at Grant Park. Rather than motor back, he chose to go by helicopter. Soon enough, however, it was time to leave the residence for the trip to the beautiful park beside Lake Michigan. For weeks, officials had been predicting that a crowd of anywhere from 500,000 to over a million would attend the Mass. Like almost everything else in Chicago, these predictions led to political controversy: a vast parking garage lies underneath Grant Park, and some people worried that the garage roof would collapse under the weight of the massive throng above. The Parks Department said it wouldn't; critics of the Parks Department said it might. At long last, an engineering firm was called in to analyze the matter; it found that the roof would not collapse. Happily, as it turned out, the firm's analysis was correct (or so it seemed, although room was left for some politician to claim that "only a miracle," presumably occasioned by the pope's presence, prevented catastrophe).

As the pope's limousine moved southward from the cardinal's residence to Grant Park, he again found the streets lined with exuberant, cheering spectators — hundreds of thousands of them. There was also a huge throng waiting at the park for him; the crowd assembled for the Mass extended over a sixteen-square-block area — farther than most eyes could see — and may have included as many as 1.5 million people. It was clearly the largest gathering that His Holiness had yet seen during his visit in the United States. There to assist the pope in serving communion to them all were priests from each Chicago parish as well as members of various religious orders.

Chicago is probably the most ethnically oriented of all American cities, and there was a one-hour program of music and pagentry before the Mass commemorating "the diverse

An artist busily sketches the scene in Grant Park.

Telephones ready for reporters on the scene

people who brought the faith to Chicago." Similarly, the pope's homily was woven skillfully and movingly around the nation's Latin motto: *E pluribus unum* ("One from many"). "When I lift up my eyes," he said to the great crowd before him, "I see in you the people of God, united to sing the praises of the Lord and to celebrate His Eucharist. I see also the whole people of America, one nation formed of many people: *E pluribus unum.*"

Holy Name Cathedral

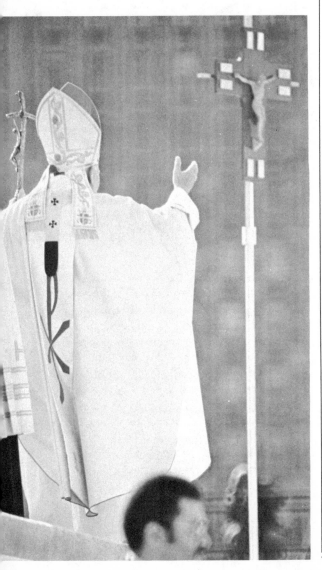

His listeners interrupted the homily with enthusiastic applause many times, punctuating the final phrases with it as John Paul quoted Christ: "'By word and example, give witness to my name / And behold, I am with you always / Until the end of the world.'" The applause took a few moments to die away, and then the pope added the one missing word: "Amen."

It was growing dark, and cold winds were whipping in off the lake as the Mass came to a close. During the ceremony, the pope often seemed overcome with intense emotion as he heard the prayers and hymns that resounded around him. When it was over, he left again for the cardinal's residence for some rest and a private dinner.

All day long, the Holy Father had been providing spiritual sustenance to others. After dinner, he had the opportunity to draw such sustenance from a source to which he often turns — music. He went to Holy Name Cathedral for a concert of sacred music by the Chicago Symphony Orchestra under Sir Georg Solti. Afterward, he stopped again to meet admiring crowds with "Sto lat!" — a Polish expression meaning "May you live a hundred years!"

Then it was back to Cardinal Cody's residence for another night of well-earned sleep. However, thousands had gathered outside the residence, and their cheers and high spirits might have kept him up all night had he not appeared on the balcony to advise them gently to go home to bed.

OCTOBER 6, 1979:
FAREWELL TO CHICAGO

The pope's departure on the morning of October 6 was efficient and unceremonious. He arose early and left the cardinal's residence by helicopter for O'Hare Airport, where he was to leave immediately on *Shepherd One* for the nation's capital. The plane was aloft and on its way by eight o'clock.

By the time he had left the Windy City, he had spent about thirty-six hours there — longer than in any of the other American cities he visited. Chicagoans like to claim that his reception in their city was the biggest, warmest (despite the chilly weather), and most enthusiastic of his week in the United States, the one that radiated the most mutual love and understanding. Many neutral observers are inclined to agree.

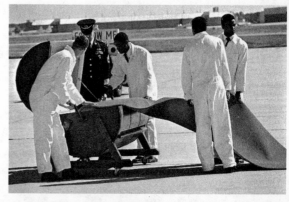

Rolling out the red carpet for the pope at the airport Below: Secret Service men survey the scene as John Paul II waves from his limousine.

OCTOBER 6, 1979:
WASHINGTON, D.C.

The pope's American pilgrimage had begun in Boston. From there, it had proceeded — with constant activity, sixteen hours a day — through the throngs of Americans who had gathered in diverse weather conditions to see him, to touch him, and to receive his blessing. He had gone among them, into the streets, the ghettos, the great sports stadiums, the cathedrals and churches, the malls and plazas. He had even gone out into the fields and farms of America. He had passed through the body of America, and had now come to the seat of this nation's government, the heart and soul of its political conscience.

John Paul II arrived from Chicago at Andrews Air Force Base. The sun was shining brilliantly, and there was a crowd of about 5,000 awaiting him. Though he was smiling and waving with as much enthusiasm as on the first day of his pilgrimage, the pope's

expression, especially around the eyes, had begun to lose much of its natural vigor; moreover, his body wasn't as upright, slumping slightly under the weight of the grueling schedules he had set for himself during the trip.

He stepped from the plane as an air force band played hymns. Vice-President Walter Mondale was there to meet him, offering the pontiff praise for having given Americans "new hope and new courage."

Boarding a marine helicopter, the papal party, now joined by William Cardinal Baum, the archbishop of Washington, was flown to the reflecting pool, which mirrors both the Lincoln and Jefferson memorials, where he began a motorcade that took him through the streets of downtown Washington to Rhode Island Avenue and Saint Matthew's Cathedral, the seat of the district's archdiocese. Outside the cathedral, a tightly packed throng of people triumphantly cheered the pontiff, overwhelming a cluster of sign-carrying demonstrators who were voicing their

Secret Service men on duty. Assignment: Shepherd

"Miz Lillian" Carter

WITH THE PRESIDENT OF THE UNITED STATES

Celebrities, members of Congress, and special guests, some 5,000 of them in all, were assembled on the north and south lawns of the White House to be introduced to John Paul II. First, His Holiness met with President Jimmy Carter in the west wing of the White House for an hour-long meeting in which there was small talk, serious talk, some picture taking, a brief tour of the White House, and then a private dialogue before the Oval Office fireplace.

On the south lawn afterward, Pope John Paul gave a statement in which he placed particular emphasis on the role the United States plays in the subjects he considers the most important of his political ministry; curtailment of the arms race, human rights, and what governments should expect of the Catholic church on these world issues. "With all my heart," he said, "I hope that there will be no relaxing of its (the United States') efforts both to reduce the risk of a fatal and disastrous worldwide conflagration and to secure a prudent and progressive reduction of the destructive capacity of military arsenals." He called on the United States — alluding as in his speech before the United Nations, to the SALT agreements — to continue forthwith its efforts to halt the arms race, making a special reference to nuclear arms. He asked that America pay heed to "the aspiration of all human beings to the full development of their capacities and the proper protection of their rights"; it would have the full cooperation of the Catholic church in "the safeguarding of the dignity of the human person and the search for justice and peace."

The pope moved away from the microphone at the conclusion of his speech. Opera star Leontyne Price sang a moving version of "The Lord's Prayer," accompanied by the National Symphony Orchestra. The pope was so overcome by this presentation that he moved back to the microphone to say, "The pope wants to bless you — with the permission of the president of the United States." It is such spontaneous remarks that have gained the pope acclaim during his appearances before the world's masses. They are the kind of repartees that have released him from the traditional constraints of previous popes and have

opposition to his policies concerning the role of women in church affairs. Inside the cathedral, the welcome was even more raucous, as thousands of clerics vociferously thrilled to the presence of their supreme leader.

John Paul took lunch in the cathedral rectory, stepping out briefly onto a balcony to wave to his admirers amassed in the street.

At 1:30 P.M., the big moment of the day arrived. The pope's motorcade, after driving slowly among the crowds lining the broad thoroughfare of Pennsylvania Avenue crying "Long live the pope!" passed through the gates of the White House for a reception given by the president of the United States.

placed him "among the people."

President Carter, too, managed to inject wit into the proceedings by departing from his prepared text, catching His Holiness slightly off guard. He stated that John Paul had come to this country "a poet, a philosopher, and a pastor." Then, pausing, he cocked his head and said, "But mostly, I think, as a pastor." Turning to the pope, smiling his famous smile, he asked, "Do you agree?"

"You are right," the pope said, nodding his head in agreement.

"He's decided not to dispute the word of the president," Mr. Carter said.

President Carter then escorted the pontiff to the reception line for introductions. VIPs in attendance included Gregory Peck, George Meany, Muriel Humphrey, Ethel Kennedy, Coretta Scott King, and the president of Notre Dame University, Theodore Hesburgh.

A memorable moment of the reception occurred when His Holiness's attention was directed to an infant in the crowd. The pope stopped, then took five-week-old Andrew Winston Stroud, son of Dr. and Mrs. Frank Stroud, in his arms and blessed him with a kiss. The Strouds explained that their son was to be baptized immediately after the White House affair.

AT THE ORGANIZATION OF AMERICAN STATES

The final event of John Paul's first day in Washington, D.C., presented him with another opportunity to speak out in favor of human rights and against nations and individuals who deny them. It happened at a special session of the Organization of American States at their headquarters in the Pan-American Building.

His remarks to this intercontinental body, whose twenty-eight ambassadors represent countries whose borders run from the northern to the southern extremes of the Western Hemisphere, were given in Spanish, the official language of that group. The remarks were short but forceful, their impact felt by those member countries whose governments abuse the rights of its citizens.

He offered praise for the organization's intent to work for the effective participation of citizens in "the responsibility and decisions" of their respective countries "through ways that take into account particular traditions, difficulties, and historical experiences."

Then, however, he admonished the membership by stating that "while such difficulties and experiences can at times call for exceptional measures and a certain period of maturation in preparation for new advances in shared responsibility, they never, never justify any attack on the inviolable dignity of the human person. If certain ideologies and certain ways of interpreting legitimate concern for national security were to result in subjugating man and his rights and dignity to the states, they would to that extent cease to be human and would be unable to claim without gross deception any Christian

Nuns listen intently to the Pope's message

Pope John Paul pauses a minute to speak with handicapped.

After the Mass on the Mall

reference." He concluded his remarks by calling on the organization to "advance a concept of the state and its sovereignty that is truly human, and that is therefore the basis for the legitimacy of the states and of their acknowledged prerogatives for the service of man."

Following a brief reception of the diplomatic corps at the Apostolic Delegation in the nation's capital, John Paul had a well-deserved night's rest.

OCTOBER 7, 1979:
EVENTS LEADING TO
THE MASS ON THE MALL

The pope's last day in the United States began at the National Shrine of the Immaculate Conception on the campus of the Catholic University of America. Here he was greeted by a thousand students who had spent the night in a prayer vigil. Telling them they were better than he for while they prayed, "I slept," the Holy Father spent close to an hour among them, creating havoc in the day's schedule.

It was during his long session with some 4,000 nuns in the Basilica that the pope was challenged by their spokeswoman, Sister Theresa Kane, a Mercy nun, president of the Leadership Conference of Women Religious to confront realistically "the great suffering of woman, particularly religious and nuns" who felt the church treated them as second-class citizens of the kingdom of God. Sister Kane told the pensive Holy Father that the church must regard the possibility of women's being included in all ministries of the church, a direct reference to the ordination of women as priests.

The Holy Father's immediate reaction was enigmatic. But when he started to speak, it was evident that he had changed his prepared text, indicating that he had seen the nun's challenge beforehand and did not prevent her from delivering the only open opposition he met with during his journey. In his long talk he gave a strong exposition of the vital part Mary had played in the history of mankind's salvation and said that nevertheless she was not among the apostles at the Last Supper, nor did she play a part in the hierarchy of the early church. He thus fended off the possibility of ordaining women.

From the shrine, Pope John Paul II stayed on campus, going to the university field house to address the nation's academic community, an ecumenical gathering at Trinity College.

Following the meeting His Holiness passed among a group of 300 handicapped persons, saying to them as he blessed them, "For you I have a special love." It was one of the more appealing moments of this populist pope's touching pilgrimage.

The evening draws to a close.

THE MASS ON THE MALL

Since dawn, people had been seeking good vantage points on the mall, a straight arrow of concrete-framed lawn and garden that stretches from the Capitol down "the Hill" to the Washington Monument. The weather had been clear earlier, promising to let people "see forever," but by afternoon and the time of the Mass, a cold wind irritated but did little to hamper the excitement of the attending crowd or the beauty of the ceremony.

In his homily, the pope spoke as a strict disciplinarian taking his cue from the Gospel text dealing with Christ's teaching on divorce and marriage. In his strongest condemnation yet of abortion, he stressed, "Human life is precious because it is the gift of a God whose love is infinite, and when God gives life, it is forever." The message was received with fervor by a large delegation of the Pro Life movement.

Bad weather and a football game interfered with attendance. The crowd anticipated at 500,000 turned out to be some 175,000.

A last look before boarding the helicopter that took him to Andrews Air Force Base and the return to Rome.

JOHN PAUL'S DEPARTURE

The Mass on the mall ended as the first clouds broke and sunshine brightened the day. At dusk, His Holiness returned to Andrews Air Force Base, where he said farewell to the United States.

"Your hospitality has been warm and filled with love, and I am grateful for all your kindness," he said, looking slightly worn and tired yet managing to leave the impression of possessing reserve energy. Assuring the American people he would always remember them in his prayers and offer them loyalty and friendship, the "new" American said, "My final prayer is this: that God will bless America, so that she may increasingly become, and truly be, and long remain, 'one nation, under God, indivisible, with liberty and justice for all.' God bless America! God bless America!"

Then he was gone. The lights of the big jet rose like a constellation of bright and guiding stars off into the dark of the night. He was gone, but never would be forgotten. John Paul II, the humble Pole, the pope of the people, all people, had accomplished his mission. He had successfully brought his presence and message to America. God had blessed America through that presence, and America had blessed God's messenger, the man who in one short year had come to represent hope to a troubled world.

A REVIEW

There can be no doubt that as a pilgrim pope, John Paul II sees the papacy in a new light. This is not just the result of his Polish ancestry and experience, but it represents a new consciousness of the pope's relation to all mankind. Taking our Lord's words to Peter literally, "But I have prayed for you that your faith may not fail, and once you have recovered, you in your turn must strengthen your brothers," he feels impelled to travel over the globe not just preaching but personally manifesting the presence of Christ; and not merely to his fellow Catholics and Christians, but to everyone, everywhere.

In the course of his first year as the Bishop of Rome and Supreme Pastor of the Catholic Church, John Paul has visited a goodly portion of his flock, and via worldwide press and TV coverage, he has been exposed to the notice of almost the whole of mankind.

Seizing the opportunity to address the General Assembly of the United Nations— an invitation extended to him by Secretary-General Kurt Waldheim, John Paul did not indulge in a perfunctory set of platitudes. Instead, he outlined realistically the dangers threatening modern civilization through a total lack of respect for human dignity and human rights caused by the greed and power-hungry ideologies struggling for world dominance. He condemned unflinchingly the dangers of international and global self-destruction now possible through nuclear armaments. Then he cited the horror of the arms race still being indulged by great and minor nations, and asked whether this was the heritage today's world wanted to hand on to its children.

John Paul's UN address was actually a political commentary on his encyclical *Redemptor Hominis (The Redeemer of Man)*. In this he maintained that the church sees Jesus Christ as a concrete historical person who plays a part in the life of every man, woman and child. Each human being is already redeemed in Christ from the "futility of creation"—the actuality of sinfulness.

It is to the individual man, woman and child that the church addresses itself when it inspires them to love both God and their neighbor. In this authentic self-love, they can slough off the tendencies to self-indulgence in greed, avarice, drugs, sexism, and other excesses that he characterized as escapist when, in Boston, he talked to the youth of America.

As he swung around the nations, the pope's message was an optimistic uplift of the ideals he seemed to exemplify in his own person. Thus in Mexico, in Poland, in Ireland, and in the United States, he was hailed not only by Catholics but by the vast majority of people as a new and welcome leader, giving new hope to this generation and this world.

In each land he seemed to realize exactly how to react to adulation, impressing people with his intense devotion to every individual who came within his gaze. He broke through the cordon of guards to touch people, pick up children, and assure one and all that he loved them. This tremendous quality of human affection simply flowed out of the Holy Father, satisfying a world hunger for reassurance that man is more than the sum of his parts; that mankind's longing for the things of the spirit did have a foundation in reality.

The Holy Father not only upheld the great spiritual values associated with their cultures and traditions, but he pointed out fearlessly the dangers and breakdowns that afflicted their people. In Mexico he condemned false ideologies based on the need for "national security," as merely a cover-up for the greed and desire to wield power that characterized so many rulers, industrialists, military cliques, and landowners.

In Poland, he challenged the Communist ideology as materialistic, degrading man's true worth under the guise of a drive for justice. At the same time, he cautioned the people about the evils of drunkenness, broken marriages, and the decadence bred by too great an interest in material well-being. But it was in the United States that he attacked most severely the evils of a purely secular society with its overindulgence in worldly goods and its relentless drive for affluence.

Among John Paul's gifts as a pastor and religious leader is his ability to bring into focus dramatically decisive incidents in the New Testament and drive home their message with startling effect. Speaking to the youth of Boston, he recreated the story of the young man who asked what he should do to obey God's will. When told to sell all he had and follow Christ, he went away sad, the Gospel says, because he had great possessions. John Paul seized upon the young man's sadness to say that true religious conviction is a thing of joy because it springs from love — the love of God and the love of neighbor — which is essentially the basis for the joyfulness of human life.

Taking the principal problems disturbing most young people — concern about their identity and worth — in his encounter with the teenagers of Madison Square Garden, John Paul evoked the experience of Saint Paul the Apostle, to insist that it was only in Jesus Christ that they would find themselves. Basing his own activities on the doings of that indefatigable traveler — "in journeys often, in perils from the sea, in danger on land" — who crisscrossed his Mediterranean world relentlessly from Tarsus to Jerusalem, from Antioch to Athens, and from Ephesus to Spain, and on to Rome, John Paul told them they should reach out to Jesus Christ who alone would give final meaning to their lives. He assured them they would find themselves in answering the needs of others — their own companions, the poor and exploited, the church and above all, in an intimacy with God, who made them with love and with joy.

That evening, recreating the Gospel parable of the rich man and Lazarus during his homily at the Mass at Yankee Stadium, John Paul zeroed in on the affluence of the United States, reminding the nation of its obligation not merely to allow the crumbs from its abundant table to provide for the poor and degraded, but that true love of neighbor means sacrifice — giving to the rest of mankind until it hurt.

This admonition John Paul had composed with enlightened self-interest at the UN speech where he insisted that failure to give to each individual the wherewithal to achieve human dignity could only bring disaster to the world.

He had a similar message for the rural world in Des Moines, Iowa, where he seemed thoroughly at home with the American farming community, a large part of the breadbasket of the world. Admiring the spiritual values that are an essential element in the cultivation of the soil, he encouraged these serious toilers of all faiths to extend their largesse to the poor and degraded people on a global scale.

But in his address in Chicago, John Paul made a great effort to demonstrate his compassionate involvement in the church's pastoral care of its people. He detailed his own experiences as parish priest and bishop as well as his involvement with Vatican Council II and the herculean effort of the church to renew itself in the contemporary world. In citing the American bishops Pastoral Letter of 1976 on the church's attitude toward "the moral life in both its individual and social aspects." John Paul went out of his way to insist upon the charity and compassion with which the law of Christ should be administered. On two topics in particular, he emphasized the wisdom of individual bishops — the condemnation of racism in all its manifestations, and the great good sense shown in adopting a truly pastoral approach to the ministry for homosexuals. But it was in his reiteration of the absolutes of Catholic sexual teaching including its current offshoot, the demand for a married clergy and women priests, that critics detected a certain lack of sensitivity on the Holy Father's part.

Thus although John Paul's visit to the United States proved a great personal triumph it left most Americans and many Catholics perplexed. There seemed a dichotomy between what he did, particularly in pleading for human dignity before the United Nations and in dealing with youth, and what he told the faithful and the bishops of the Catholic church. People were puzzled when in his address to the hierarchy in Chicago and in his homily at the Mass on the Washington Mall he expressed little of the personal compassion for sinners and suffering humanity that he exhibited in person to all he encountered.

In reiterating the church's teaching on moral problems, John Paul spoke of the great pastoral charity that should animate bishops and priests in expounding God's law. But then he seemed, as several commentators remarked, to resort to a benevolent but strait-laced moralism by quoting from a pastoral document published by the American bishops several years ago. He praised the pastoral letters of American bishops that condemned racism and gave spiritual consolation to the homosexual. But then, instead of enunciating the religious and ethical obligations of the Christian life in a truly conciliatory fashion, conscious of the human weakness and the social and economic circumstances that caused these obligations to be violated, he seemed to be misled into pious and moralistic reassertion, particularly in his homily in Washington. This approach shocked many of his Catholic faithful, upset other Christians, and bewildered the outside world, all of whom are seeking a humane — hence moral — answer to the problems affecting millions of men and women suffering the effects of original sin.

No one expected the pope to take a different stance on abortion, extramarital sex, artificial birth control, married clergy in the Western church, the ordination of women priests, or the dangers of self-indulgence. But many hoped that he would deal with the other aspects of these problems that are being wrestled with so desperately by clergy, nuns, and laity on the pastoral level. It is these apostles of the concrete individual who need encouragement and recognition.

In place of branding married couples generally for using contraception, commentators felt that he might have inquired why millions of good Catholics found themselves bound in conscience to limit their families. He might have read them the Vatican Council's benevolent advice that "realizes that modern conditions often keep couples . . . in circumstances where at least temporarily the size of their family should not be enlarged . . . where the intimacy of married love is broken off, it is not rare for its faithfulness to be imperiled . . . then the upbringing of children and the courage to have more are both endangered."
(Gaudium et Spes No. 51)

In the larger perspective John Paul II in Chicago seemed to ignore what he said in Philadelphia on human dignity: "human Christian values are fostered when every effort is made so that no child anywhere in the world faces death because of a lack of food, or faces a diminished intellectual and physical potential for want of sufficient

nourishment, or has to bear all through life the scars of deprivation."

Since at least one third of the world's children do not enjoy these "human Christian values" — Robert McNamara of the World Bank maintains that thirty million children under five die of starvation each year — critics wanted to know how their parents and the people attempting to assist them, can be accused of a procontraception mentality when they feel conscience-bound to limit their families?

On divorce, the Holy Father again seemed to miss a great opportunity. He failed to encourage the millions of Catholics and other like-minded people, and their counselors, both clerical and lay, to try to salvage broken marriages, to delve into the sacramental and societal remedies for the hopelessly alienated, and to give new stimulus to the preparation of bride and groom for the burdens as well as the divine gift of love without which, again according to Vatican Council II, there can be no marriage. There seemed to be some distance between the pope's proclamation of an intense papal desire for Christian unity and his intransigent stand against intercommunion.

While the Holy Father has frequently identified himself with the accomplishments of the Vatican Council on its great Pastoral Constitution on the Church in Today's World, he seemed to have obscured its significance in dealing with the specific issues troubling the American church in both his talks to the bishops in Chicago and his final sermon at the Mass on the mall in the nation's capital.

Where this phenomenon came to the surface was in John Paul's insistence on the necessity of preserving the church's doctrines intact — a worry that he allowed himself to be persuaded was a principal concern for American Catholics. Actually, it has been described as a major preoccupation of bishops who are negating their obligation to get down to the concrete problems of pastoral concern. In any case, John Paul insisted that Pope John XXIII's principal purpose for calling Vatican Council was "that the sacred deposit of Christian doctrine should be more effectively guarded and taught."

In so saying, John Paul II was somewhat less than accurate. In his speech opening the council, John XXIII said explicitly: "The salient point of the council is not, therefore, a discussion of one article or another of the fundamental doctrine of the faith. For this a council was not necessary. . . . But the Christian and apostolic spirit of the whole world expects a step forward toward a doctrinal penetration and a formation of consciences. . . . The substance of the ancient doctrine of the deposit of faith is one thing; and the way it is presented is another." It is this last sentence that prevailed in the council's accomplishments introducing development and therefore change in many of the church's modes of conceiving its doctrines and moral directives. For this reason many troubled pastors and counselors were expecting the Holy Father to aid them in a more realistic application of the church's teaching on these difficult problems.

In his talk to the academic community, at Catholic University the pope did actually give encouragement to the theologians, assuring them of their worth and insisting that they employ objective, in-depth methods in their search for an updating of church teaching. At the same time he instructed the bishops to perform their function of safe-guarding true doctrine and instructing the faithful as is their fundamental task.

Appearing as an incomparable personality — handsome, powerful, dynamic, with a thespian feel for language, and mesmeric ability to fascinate a crowd, Pope John Paul simply overwhelmed the majority of his vast audiences. He thrilled the Mexicans, reconquered the Poles, fascinated the Irish, and beguiled the Americans by his indefatigable interest in people, his genuine love of children, and his responsive reassurance to everyone seeking his attention.

Unconscious of the popery antipathy that affected America down to at least World War I, the people in the streets and the molders of public opinion welcomed the dynamic strapping figure in the white cassock and round, red Roman hat, whose incredible itinerary through their cities took up so much of the TV and radio time during the day, and overwhelmed the news programs in the evening.

Observers agreed that the Holy Father has in mind unifying a church primarily through his personal charisma which he intends to use in contacting the faithful and the secular all over the globe. At the same time he seems determined to restore the old certainties in the moral order as a counter force to the breakdown of decency and morality now affecting world society.

Most people feel that this is a noble objective. But many feel that unhappily the new pope has not yet had time to view the specific problems of humanity and of the church from the vantage point of a universal pastor. Apparently conscious of the unhappy reaction to some of his pronouncements John Paul admitted that "as we proclaim the truth in love, it is not possible for us to avoid all criticism; or to please everyone. But it is possible for us to work for everyone."

As the Holy Father took to the skies for his return to the Eternal City he left behind him a slightly bewildered American Catholic Church. As pope, he felt he had to be the conserver of tradition. Hence no one should have expected him to introduce major changes in the teachings and moral directives considered accepted doctrine by his immediate predecessors and the majority of the faithful.

As his voyagings indicated, Pope John Paul intended to give the church a new vision of the papacy. He felt it his duty not merely to announce the good news of the Gospel, but to give personal witness as a man endowed by the Spirit and called to represent Jesus Christ to all of mankind.

Americans along with the rest of the world could not help but love this indefatigable talker who responded to the chant, "John Paul II, we love you!" with the reply: "John Paul II, he loves you!"

It was with the permission of President Carter that John Paul gave his blessing to the statesmen and notables who met him in the White House garden. And it was with the permission of the Commander of Andrews Air Force Base that he finally took off for Rome, a tired but totally satisfied Holy Father. This man of God had the unique satisfaction of winning the respect and love of a great number of Americans whom he added to the millions of Mexicans, Poles, and Irish who felt such genuine affection for the pilgrim pope. Arriving home in Vatican City, he said simply, "America has done well by this pope!"

Only the immediate future will show whether his double level approach will succeed. Meanwhile he had the adoring affection of the millions whom he charmed with his gracious, shrewd, warm, humorous, Christ-oriented personality.

F. X. Murphy, C.SS.R.
Holy Redeemer College
Washington, D.C.